the story of US

the story of US

Infinite Joy

A NOVEL

DR. LYNDA BOUCUGNANI-STOUT

Reimagined Thought
PUBLISHING

Dedication

THIS BOOK IS DEDICATED to all the great teachers of the world which includes those of us in everyday life, those who have influenced us through the ages, those who have taught us through our spiritual souls, and even storytellers and movie makers who have condensed essential truths to the printed word or a graphic illustration. These great teachers all have a few things in common. They care about others, they are open to possibilities, they constantly want to learn more and they are empathetic and kind. They often put others before themselves, are never quick to judge, want to encourage others and have the most positive motivation for what they do. They prioritize true caring and helping over personal gain—always. They are a treasure.

It is also dedicated to those of us who have struggled to find true love, feel the emptiness of not having it, and often blame ourselves for not feeling it in our lives. Sometimes we need to take the time and self-reflect to understand real love, what it is and what it is not in order to find our own path. Through this story it is hoped that others can take this journey of self-awareness, find what is important to them, be brave, and perhaps find the love they have been longing for all their lives. Only then can they fully appreciate its majesty.

Special Thanks

My greatest thanks goes to my husband, affectionately known as Obi Wan Kenobi, without whom this book would not exist. We have learned so much together, have endured so much, and through constant introspection and the best communication in the world, truly understand what love really is and what it is not. You are a great teacher, wise and so kind to everyone around you. You are my life, my everything, I adore you and the fantastic person you are.

Very special thanks to my two "first" readers for their support, understanding, wonderful feedback and enduring friendship: Theresa Slavic and Matt Finn. They are both exceptionally good people, definitely members of the Good People Club, and a delight to be around.

Special acknowledgments and thanks go to my content editor, Debbie Ihler Rasmussen; my proofing and copy editor, and eBook designer, Kim Autrey; and my book cover and interior book designer Francine Platt at Eden Graphics, Inc.

HOME SWEET HOME

Dear Reader,

BEFORE STARTING ON THE NOVEL, I encourage you to carefully read the **Prelude** to *The Story of US*. These are questions which could potentially be answered by reading this book. Take the time to decide for **yourself**, which ones are most important for you. In this way you will not only understand what to expect but also to relate your own life to the words you read in the book, and the situations that occur. Think about highlighting or writing down those questions that resonate the most with you personally.

This story begins "In the Dimension of Heaven." There are vivid descriptions of what it is like there. All of this comes from the scientific study of Near-Death Experiences, a particular focus of mine over the past forty plus years. They are not my idea of what heaven is like but actual descriptions of people who have died, reported that they went to heaven, and then reported what they saw, heard, and felt. I was fortunate to meet with Dr. Raymond Moody on several occasions and discuss this new discovery. He coined the words "near death experiences" in his pivotal book in 1976, *Life After Life*. Since that time, it has exploded in scientific awareness and study that merges with spiritual understanding.

Starting in heaven is necessary since it is the place where the two main characters first knew each other, at the time they decided to come back to Earth to learn more—through direct experience. Although they didn't know it at the time, their mission was to learn what real love is and what it is not.

This is an epic story covering over seventy years of their individual lives on Earth for this mission and all their experiences throughout this time. One wonders, "Did they ever meet up here on Earth?" If so, "Did they fully learn what true love is—and what it is not?" And "What can we learn from them—what can they teach us?"

I would love to hear from you after reading this book. Please visit my author website at drlyndaauthor.com and leave a review. Enjoy.

Blessings,

Lynda

The Story of US
Infinite Joy

A NOVEL BASED ON A TRUE STORY

DID YOU KNOW that soulmates originate in the dimension of heaven? • Have you ever wondered what true love really is? • Do you know the meaning—the purpose of life on Earth? • What is the difference between pretend love, wishful thinking love and true deep love? • What do we really know about what heaven is? • Is there a reason why some people experience deep tragedies in their lives? • What is the first thing you must have if you want deep true love with another person? • What effect can childhood trauma have on a person throughout their lives? • What is a good person? • How is independence and self-reliance developed in a person? • What can you learn by examining another's motivation in life? • What is the advantage of sticking to your own principles? • How does one survive multiple tragedies and great loss in their life? • Just what is happiness? • Do you believe that coincidence is God's way of staying anonymous? • Should one stay in a non-marriage and be unhappy for the rest of their life? • What are the ways one often protects when faced with constant pain and unhappy relationships? • Is it best for love to start slow and grow over time and connection? • What characterizes the deepest, most true love imaginable? • Can a person in her seventies really feel like a teenager? • Why is it important to learn what love is not? • Are you known and accepted for just who you are? • What is the most important emotion we should seek while we are here on Earth?

Dr. Lynda's description of the Dimension of Heaven
is based on a more than 4 decade scientific study
of near-death experiences.

In the Dimension
of Heaven

WITH PERFECT HARMONY, tinkling bells swayed with blades of lush, emerald-green grass. Forests of majestic symmetrical trees all synchronized as if an orchestra of sounds, joy, and beauty, beyond any earthly description. Endless pathways evoked all senses and filled one's spirit with immense love and appreciation.

Mystical colors in every direction, so vibrant and diverse, unlike anything seen on Earth. Colors like velvet seemingly liquid and full of light coming from everywhere and absorbed by everything they touched. In full display, flowers of the most magnificent colors never encountered on Earth and were incredible. The entire surroundings filled one's soul with immense pleasure and an awareness that love included beauty, for it could caress the soul.

Flowers swayed in time with the most incredible music; unlike anything you had ever heard. One could walk right over the flowers, and they were never damaged. It was like walking on love. If you picked a flower, immediately a new one would grow in its place. Everything seemed more real than on Earth, and one feels more alive than they have ever been.

In this place of love, you may feel that you've existed forever. The leaves of trees made sounds of chimes as they brushed against one another with the pleasant breeze. If you picked a fruit from any of the trees close to you, another would grow in its place.

In this dimension of heaven, there is no death as we know it. The air is infused with the most delectable of aromas that breathe peace, love, and contentment. A desired taste would evaporate on your tongue with the most spectacularly delicious, unimaginable flavor, though you may not recognize it. Heavenly beings don't require food or drink, because all energy comes from God in the form of light, but they can if they so desire.

Vision in the heavenly dimension is extraordinary; even if you had problems seeing, or were blind on Earth, your vision is telescopic here. You can see for miles from wherever you are. Things are clear, precise, and enhanced, with a range of colors unimaginable. The skies are like velvet, and you may see some spiritual beings, perhaps angels who live in their own realm but can appear as human or shine exquisitely with radiant, mesmerizing light. You may also see orbs of light shining with a golden hue.

Everything is more here, including your thinking. In the heavenly dimension, you will communicate with others by telepathy, there is no need to speak. Your thoughts come to you very rapidly, like the speed of light. If you have questions, answers are immediate; you will never be put on hold.

Time in the heavenly dimension is not as it is on Earth. It is non-linear. Both time and space are altered. As compared with human minds, a minute can seem like a lifetime, and a lifetime or multiple lifetimes can seem like just a moment in time.

In heaven, the natural way of physical movement is somewhat like flying, only immediate. One only has to think of where they want to go, and in an instant, they are there. However, if they choose to go slowly, they can do that too. There is still free will in heaven. Your thoughts come to you very rapidly, like the speed of light. You don't need to eat or drink in the heaven dimension because all energy comes from God in the form of light.

On Earth, God has provided us with the incredible knowledge of the heavenly dimension through other's near-death experiences; a gift to learn from those who have clinically died and came back to life. In nearly all cases, the experience totally changed their lives. These NDE's (Near-Death Experiences) have been the study of scientists for several decades, and it has been found that much of it coincides with scripture and teachings from various religious orientations.

Often individuals transitioning from Earth to the heavenly dimension report vivid accounts of what they have seen and heard. Individuals who died on the operating table, for example, often report traveling up to the ceiling where they observe their own body being operated on and can later recall exactly what individual professionals were saying and doing from that perspective. They were able to travel through ceilings, and some have even reported seeing items on the roofs of hospitals that are later verified. They usually encounter some sort of barrier before entering heaven, and some, but not all, report going through a dark tunnel with the speed of light. Along the way, they may see deceased relatives or spirits as if accompanying them on their journey.

There is generally a perception of an immense, brightly shining light that beckons them. Most describe an enormous feeling of love, peace, and tranquility unlike anything they have ever felt before. Very frequently they note waves of pure, unconditional love and enormous joy. They may see a being shining brighter than the sun, but they are still able to look upon it. This being radiates powerful love, acceptance, and compassion beyond all imaginings.

Some of those who experience near-death, then encounter a life review. It is rather like a panorama of continuous life events of the individual, moving at exceptional speed, but they are, somehow, able to comprehend two things. First, to see what they did in their life and second, to *feel, actually experience* how the individual or individuals they interacted with in life felt about their actions.

It appears that it will be an enormous learning experience for anyone. At some point, they reach a stage where they have to decide. They may be told that they need to go back to Earth because it is not their time, and there is still much for them to do. Many times, they are given a choice because there is still free will. It is often agonizing to make such a choice because they don't want to leave this heavenly place so full of love and joy. But thankfully, these people can help all of us to understand what happens when we actually die. What we can look forward to.

Most individuals who have a near-death experience and who have advanced to this stage report encountering many people, including deceased loved ones and others they had known throughout their own Earth life experiences. They would appear as they did in their earthly bodies but can also have different forms in heaven. Typically, a new person in the heavenly realm is able to recognize their loved ones. They will see that they still have a body, but it is different. Bodies in heaven may be almost transparent, those who have a near-death experience may see through the body, even to objects that may be on the other side of it.

When going to this heavenly dimension, the individuals' report that they retain their identity as on Earth. This would include their unique personality, their sense of humor, their look, and their emotions. However, now they will be able to be themselves—at last. They will learn just who God intended for them to be. We are all here for a specific purpose. Love is always a major part of that purpose, no matter what our other earthly accomplishments may be.

Imagine, when you enter the heavenly dimension, you continue on your journey through the pathway. You will likely encounter a great city—but it will be different from any city you have seen before. Imagine a city the size of the entire Earth, full of what we need to give us unimaginable joy. Whatever you need to feel joy, you will have. Continued learning is a major part of the heavenly dimension. You may see libraries of knowledge and a library with the records of the life reviews of all who have come there.

Many who come to the heavenly dimension will be happy to stay in the entry realm of this new home. Think of heaven as a series of concentric half circles or sections of the earth's atmosphere. The lowest level is the one you first enter, and it is glorious. However, some will want to go higher, to get as close to where God is as possible. He/she is at the very top. In order to do that, one must learn more, sometimes coming back to Earth to do so. It seems there are also ways to advance learning within the heavenly realm without coming back, which would explain why there are so many places of learning there.

A beautiful bench near a park finds two *residents* of this dimension of heaven. They often liked to be together, and this was a favorite spot. From this vantage point they could look out over the universes while simultaneously enjoying the beauty of the park full of flowers of every shape and size, grasses that swayed and waved in the golden glow of their home. Sometimes the grass sounded like bells tinkling, and other times it would hum, or even join in with a chorus of music coming from somewhere.

On this day the couple took the form of their Earth bodies which were in the prime of their lives when they had previously lived on Earth. At other times they may choose to be golden orbs. They make their choice based on what appeals to them each day. They had a specific reason for this today, they would decide if they would return to Earth for another lifetime. They were to teach others about true love and gratitude. They had more life to live; they hoped to greatly advance their understanding of Love.

Depending on what souls were trying to accomplish in the heavenly dimension, they may be studying to learn necessary truths in order to advance and to be in closer connection with God. This is a major quest for many in this realm, though not all. There are myriad ways to learn, actual academies where souls sometimes take the form of golden orbs. They can merge for a time into one as they learn important points to build their souls and collective consciousness. Then they can go back to their individual selves again.

All knowledge is available in the heavenly dimension, but each soul must take the initiative; it's a choice. Some are ecstatically happy in the entry level of the heavenly dimension, after all, it's more glorious than anything they have ever experienced before. If they decide to stay in that level, it is alright, but they are encouraged to keep learning. However, unconditional love flows into each soul wherever they are in the heavenly dimension. Within the realm of the immense city with its layers of beauty and knowledge, there are places where one can learn about a multiple of subjects, see art galleries, museums, gorgeous fountains, rivers and lakes, waterfalls, musical events, even games and sports activities.

This is real, true life in the dimension of heaven. Souls may want to continue learning in a field or an interest they had while on Earth or explore something new. It's all available. No one is bored in this dimension. There are responsibilities and roles for each soul. There is endless creation, and so there is constant research, discovery, and creating going on. There are also infinite mysteries of both Earth and all of the universes that are impossible to know and explore to completion. However, the biggest reward in this heavenly dimension is intimacy with God. That is why some choose to develop further to get as close to the realm of God as possible.

The warmth, love beyond words that flows from the divine being toward souls entering this dimension is like a magnet that cannot be resisted. This divine being, or God, is responsible for all creation. The most magnificent love, beauty, majestic creations that are beyond our capacity to imagine. Pure joy, pure contentment, and pleasure are all there. No wonder souls seek to be as close to God as possible.

These two souls sit on the bench, they see their beloved earthly dogs, running through fields toward them. Pets are there to love and cherish for eternity for all souls who want to be with them. Many other animals are there as well, and the children especially love to be with them. Animals all live in harmony with one another; there is nothing but love. Souls who come to the heavenly dimension as children will continue to grow in this dimension, both physically in appearance, and in learning. They have the capability to appear to new loved ones coming into the heavenly dimension in the way they would be most recognized by those newcomers.

Love is the main eternal focus of God.

These two souls have decided to return to Earth. They hope to perfect their understanding of Love. They have both advanced beyond their current understanding.

But it is not enough.

To truly learn they must experience what true love really is—*and what it is not*. The three key points are *experience*; what true love feels like on Earth, and very importantly, what it is not. This can only happen by returning to Earth and living lives there.

Both of these souls are already *teachers* in this heavenly dimension. Their roles are to help others learn and understand all about love, especially unconditional love. The decision was an easy one for them, as they both always want to be the best they can be. They are very close and have a lot in common. They have a strong motivation to help others.

These two souls are about to embark on the most significant experience in their entire soul development. Both are aware that they are likely to have very difficult and even heart-wrenching experiences on Earth, but they also know that what they will learn will be exhilarating, powerful, incredibly fulfilling and so look forward to teaching this to others.

They have been told that while on Earth, they will have no recollection of being in the heavenly dimension and will be born at different times; they are also advised they may not even encounter one another.

On Earth, such individuals are often referred to as *soulmates;* an apt description for these two.

First you must conceive
Then you must believe
Then and only then
can you achieve
- ROBBIE

Robbie

This first memory remains embedded in Robbie's five-year-old brain and will impact him for the rest of his life. The sheer beauty of the setting screams for recognition but is hijacked by the blatant terror of what happened to him.

Robbie carefully studied a salamander navigating its murky surroundings. He sat close to the bubbling stream near the alcove at the edge of the deep river. He could hear the laughter of his brothers swimming and frolicking in the water as if they had no care in the world.

But Robbie stayed by the safety of the stream. He loves the outdoors, and he calls the salamander Charlie; he wants to protect him. Robbie is curious and tries to understand the world. He loves the mountains, rivers, creeks, and lakes.

A loud, disdaining voice shouts at him from behind the rocks at the edge of the river.

A dark shadow called harshly, "Come here, boy! What are you doing just sitting there? You should be swimming just like your brothers!"

Robbie hesitantly moved toward the monster. "But I don't know how to swim."

"Get over here. I'll teach you how to swim!"

Robbie wanted to shrink deeper into the mud, but he doesn't dare. He stood before the *teacher*. He is afraid to move.

"You just walk into the water and start to move your hands and legs. It's so simple any baby could do it."

What is the worst danger? The monster or the deep river behind me?

He didn't have time to answer his own question. Quicker than his friend Charlie could run, he was roughly pulled off the ground by the monster and was thrown into the deep water.

"That's it! Now go swim! That will teach you how to swim, boy."

Terrified, Robbie gulped for air.

I'm going to die!

Swept away by the current, he thinks of his mother, the one person he knows really loves him. If only he could be in her arms.

He slowly sinks deeper, and his body eases itself into acceptance; he is hardly moving at all now. He is fascinated; he can see things with his open eyes that are new to him and even spark a sense of wonder.

Suddenly, Robbie is jerked from the water by his older brother, Adam, who drags him to the river bank. Gasping for air, he sees the concern on the faces of all his brothers who are gathered around him. Through blurred eyes, he catches a glimpse of his father, who, characteristically, turned his back and walked away, not doing anything. He was so self-absorbed, he couldn't see the goodness of his sons, or anyone around him.

This memory and many similar others would emotionally haunt Robbie throughout his life—*until it didn't.*

Jeanette

JEANETTE'S EARLY CHILDHOOD seemed ideal, and in many respects, it was. But lurking beneath were substantial anxieties and related events that influenced her life well into adulthood. Jeanette spent a lot of her time outdoors, but she also enjoyed being alone. She loved to imagine, even creating plays that she and her friends could perform, and she often explored various unknown places in the woods next to her house; usually alone, hoping to conquer some of her fears. She liked to remember being in the nice house she lived in with her mother, father, older brother Josh, and their remarkable grandmother, she referred to as Gram.

Not even Jeannette's parents knew of the vivid thoughts and anxieties that coursed through her brain and the impact they had in her daily life. She appeared to be carefree, but some family members saw her as being on the anxious side. They didn't see what she felt every day when she was outside playing with her friends. Jeanette kept everything to herself—the beginnings of the very independent person she was to become.

White cement trucks would sometimes go through her neighborhood to and from the concrete factory near her suburban home. Jeanette felt an overwhelming need to hide from those trucks. She became very quick and vigilant. She knew exactly where to hide from them. Sometimes it was the big hill in her friend Pat's front yard; hiding behind a house was another go-to spot.

She wasn't sure why she felt compelled to hide, but she didn't want to find out what would happen to her if one of them saw her. And she kept it a secret from her friends and her parents. Why in the world did she do this? She was too young to figure it out, and besides, she was embarrassed by it.

Jeanette also often had recurring dreams about being captured by the moon and a sinister character dressed in black with a crooked hat and a crooked smile. He seemed to be acting on Earth at the moon's command. These dreams affected her everyday life too. Convinced that if the moon caught her outside after dark, it would suck her up and she would be gone forever.

Consequently, she was always vigilant about being home before dark. She shared bunk beds with her brother Josh, and she was careful to make sure she could not be seen by the moon through the bedroom window by covering it with a towel. This went on for many years, but Jeanette never whispered her reality to anyone.

She adored her dad, admired her mom, and loved her older brother, Josh, who was often her protector. One time her friend Pat took her doll and insisted that it was hers. Jeanette and Pat had a love/hate relationship. Jeanette always felt in competition with her, and that she didn't measure up, but she always wanted to.

Josh just marched down to Pat's house and demanded the doll back. He followed her right to her room, retrieved the doll, and brought it back to his sister. He gave her a hug.

Josh made her feel safe; he stood up for her.

Jeanette liked to be given responsibility, fulfill expectations, and perform well. When she was eight, she established a clinic for little pets in Pat's basement, and all the neighborhood kids would bring their pets to her clinic. Some dogs and cats, but mainly little bugs, caterpillars, fish, salamanders, turtles, an occasional bird, rabbit, or whatever her friends wanted to be healed.

Jeanette loved this. Her favorite TV show was *Marcus Welby, MD* who had his office right in his home. She wanted to be just like him.

On one occasion when Jeanette was nine years old, her teacher gave her a job. She was to report to the parents of two little girls who lived near her, that they were stuck at school after a snowstorm.

No more buses could get out on the road. The bus taking Jeanette home went up the hill, and she saw another bus going down the hill. She had to get off a little early to report to the parents. Within seconds of getting off the bus, she heard a loud crash. She looked down the hill at the commotion. For a second, Jeanette didn't know what to do, so she ran down the hill. She discovered a little girl wearing a red coat had been hit by the school bus. She was laying in the snow, her head on a helmet that was filling up with red blood.

Jeanette wanted her mom but remembered her mission and rushed back up the hill to go to the house of the stranded little girls who were still at school. There were steep concrete steps going down a hill to the front door of their house. She started down but slipped and fell down the steps, but she made it to the door, told the mom, and then started to walk home.

Her mom worked for the police department, and Jeanette learned later that when her mom heard of the bus accident, she was frantically trying to get there because she was afraid it was Jeanette.

There was always a lot going on in Jeanette's mind. Though she didn't remember why, somehow, the color red was always there.

Family life was good. Until it wasn't.

Sages

Whenever souls went to Earth to learn and evolve, they are each assigned a sage to watch over them. The sage takes notes of how experiences affect and mold them into who they were meant to be. Often not an easy road, it was important for the sages to have a constant view and understanding of how their growth was progressing.

Robbie's sage was Sage Franklin and Jeanette's, Sage Ellie. Just like the souls they were watching, sages have their own personalities. Vivacious and outspoken, Ellie is attentive and funny with a slant to the sarcastic side.

Franklin may be described as *measured*, one who would wisely consider his words. He had a subdued sense of humor, was thoughtful and slightly *snarky.*

Both Franklin and Ellie were empathetic, an essential quality for all sages.

Franklin sighed. "It's amazing how that one event when Robbie was five years old could have such an impact on his personality."

Ellie nodded. "I was so mad at his father. I wanted to throw *him* in the river!"

"Ellie, you know that's not our purpose here. We are to watch over their growth and development. Only when we see something extremely wrong in their journey do we alert the Boss."

"But what a horrid thing to do to a child. That father is a fake. He appears totally different to others in the community; charming and successful. But where is his heart with his family?"

"Jeanette has some underlying child issues too, but of a different nature," said Franklin. "She is an independent, imaginative, and introspective child. But she has lived with a fear and has no idea where it came from. Sometimes not knowing can be worse."

"It will definitely shape her life, especially since she won't figure it out until she is in her forties. She is responsible and takes that very seriously. She's the opposite of carefree."

"Yes, and besides responsibility, she has such a high level of empathy for a little one."

"Both of them will need some strong examples in their lives to help them stay on track," said Ellie. "Their life events, though carefully designed for maximum growth, will be hard, but similar in nature. We'll have fun watching this, and I imagine we'll learn a thing or two from them as well."

Robbie

ROBBIE'S FATHER, Clarence, got up early and headed for his furniture store. He went inside the office and sat at his desk. He rarely talked to his family. He might say something disparaging to his wife, but he never offered any warm feelings.

The middle of seven children, Robbie did things with his brothers and one sister. They lived in a rural area with little in the way of amenities but did have a nice house in a beautiful countryside.

Clarence's routine after work was to eat dinner, park himself in his den with a bottle of whiskey and sit in front of the TV for the rest of the evening. He rarely interacted with others in the family aside from tossing out hurtful, belittling words.

Robbie had never trusted his father, but he always trusted his mom. His mother loved her kids, and they loved her back, especially Robbie. He admired his mom and had a secure connection with her. He loved spending time with her and loved playing Scrabble with her—she always told him, "You may win, but I'm not going to LET you win."

Robbie's mother, Violet, was kind. People looked up to her and respected the way she treated others. No one ever knew that her husband called her a "fat ass" in front of the children.

In this tiny town, Robbie and his brothers usually spent most of their free time together. When they were old enough, each was recruited to help at the store. Growing up in this environment, his older brothers drank—a lot, and his favorite uncle was drunk when he fell and drowned in a river.

Robbie was an intelligent child with a love for learning—especially reading. When he was in the fifth grade he was asked to join a group of older kids for special instruction with reading and literature. Most were in the eighth grade. Robbie had no idea what was expected of him, but he went. They met in a dilapidated church that was right next to the school. The paint was peeling and it smelled old—and musty. Perhaps the forebear of gifted education that would come later.

When Robbie entered high school, he became less interested in schoolwork but did enjoy the high school experience. He never once went out on a date, and he *never* did homework; he didn't have to study. Robbie always wanted to make people laugh, earning him the reputation of class clown, to him this was his only badge of honor.

Robbie's relationship with his father never improved, and he knew his brothers felt the same way. Robbie would often say about his father, "He never said a good word about me in his life."

It was an immense, ugly boulder on his back causing resentment and hatred to grow within him. On one occasion, one of his brothers said to all of them, "Do you hate Dad?" and they *all* shouted, "Hell, Yes!"

When Robbie was in his senior year in high school, his father's business burned down. Clarence managed to keep the business running, from a tiny building he used as his office, but he had nowhere to display furniture. It was up to Robbie and his three older brothers to rebuild the building with a hired carpenter to supervise. Robbie had just finished high school, and for their work they each received a pittance each week. Their dad never told any of them thank-you.

Robbie didn't want to work with his dad, so after graduation he started looking for a job. On one especially hot and sticky summer evening, he went into his father's office. Clarence glared at his son in a state of fury. Apparently, he had seen a tiny dent on the pickup truck the boys used in rebuilding the store and attacked Robbie for his carelessness and failure to inform him. This was much more than a reprimand, it was an opportunity to berate Robbie for over an hour letting him know how worthless he was, and that he would never amount to anything. He wouldn't stop, and at this time, in this part of the country, the worst thing a kid could do was talk back to any grown up, but *especially* his father.

Finally, Robbie lost it. He jabbed his finger in his father's face. "YOU SHUT THE FUCK UP!"

Stunned, Clarence balled up his fist and reared back, ready to strike Robbie.

But Robbie stood his ground. "You hit me, and I will fuckin' kill you." He turned on his heel and walked out the door.

He never looked back.

Robbie walked the sidewalks of the minuscule town. He knew he couldn't go home but didn't know where to go. By luck, he ran into his cousin who told him about an opportunity to apply for a job in Baltimore, Maryland, with the B and O railroad. It was some distance away, and his cousin advised they had to apply on Monday, in just two days. With no transportation, only the clothes on his back, and less than ten dollars in his wallet, he decided to hitchhike.

He got the job, and at seventeen, this was the beginning of his independence.

The railroad job was hard, physical work, and after about six months, the railroad began moving operations to another area, and Robbie was laid off.

He learned about a possible new job in a town not too far away from his hometown in a sprawling, formidable-looking rayon factory. He called his mom to tell her this, and she told him he could live at the big house in a room on the second floor.

"You don't even have to see him, Robbie. There is no reason for you to talk with him or interact with him in any way," said Mom. "I miss you, Robbie."

So, Robbie moved back in.

The rayon factory was huge—an immense building where different aspects of rayon manufacturing took place in different sections. Being a newbie, no one envied the job he was given. He was charged with making sure the small chemical chunks used to make the product when mechanically dumped into the huge, tube-shaped railroad cars, didn't stick to the walls. To do this he used a huge fork-like tool, climbed down a ladder through a hole in the top, and scraped the sides. Most of the material would start to build up first in the middle, at the bottom of the car, and Robbie had to have one hand on the ladder while using the other to maneuver the tool.

He climbed down the ladder to the floor of the railroad car and was immediately overwhelmed by the hundred-degree heat, and he choked on the sickening smell. At first, he was doing okay. He held onto the ladder with one hand and shook residue off the sides with the other; it was so hot and claustrophobic. Suddenly, there was an odd, creaking sound, and the whole mechanism that fed the chemical chunks collapsed, knocking him off the ladder.

Gasping for air, Robbie struggled to get to his feet. He was surrounded by chemical chunks that were already at his neck deep. He scrambled to find the ladder, his only chance of getting out. The chunks kept coming, and he couldn't see.

I don't want to die. Dear Lord, help me find the ladder.

"Help! Someone, help!"

He knew no one could hear him. No one else was around.

The company sent workers down into the hot, thermos-shaped railroad cars alone.

Safety was not a priority.

Robbie kept groping and finally found the metal of the ladder. He used both hands to pull himself up on it and started the difficult climb.

Finally, he reached the opening, tumbled out, and gulped in air.

"I'm never doing this again," he choked.

Robbie decided then and there that he needed to get an education. He realized he would have to do this on his own.

So, he did.

Jeanette

An intelligent and creative man, Jeanette's dad, George, enjoyed inventing new things; mechanical tools and devices, beautiful gardens and ponds. Handsome and endearing, he gave Jeanette joy and comfort when she was a child.

She remembered riding her bike and falling off, crashing to the road, landing in gravel. Her dad came running out of the house, scooped her up, and carried her home. She remembered she was wearing a navy-blue dress with white trim, and it became almost like a permanent photo embedded in her brain.

One time after a particularly good snowfall, her dad built a huge toboggan that would fit all of the family and a few more. He scoured around for the best sleighing spot and settled in on an actual street with an enormous hill that ended into another crosswise street. Off they went, the whole family. Jeanette was a little scared hoping there would be no cars at the bottom of the hill, but she trusted in her father. She had so much fun that day because she trusted her dad.

Jeanette's dad and mom married just after he returned from World War II where he was assigned to Pearl Harbor. When the bombing started, he and two friends came out of the mess hall, found a rickety old machine gun in an adjacent building, and began firing on the planes. It was brutal. The planes were firing on them, but the rickety old gun persevered. Three heroes, but one of them was killed that day. George received a Purple Heart and other medals for his time in the war which later included Okinawa and islands around Japan. Jeanette's dad worked for AT&T (the beginnings of the company) after the war, first as a lineman and later in various roles inventing new ways of doing things and solving problems.

Jeanette's mom, beautiful Belle, was described by others as vivacious, fun, always delightful to be around, and flirtatious in nature. She seemed to love life, was a people-person, and always had a smile on her face. Once the kids were in school, she worked at various jobs; secretary at the police department, and a salesperson in the glove department at a department store. Typical for their time, neither Belle nor George had any education beyond high school.

Jeanette's beloved Gram lived with them, and eventually, she and Gram shared a bed and large bedroom. She would watch her Gram get on her knees every night and pray; the night was less scary with her Gram. She was the one who provided most of Jeanette's spiritual, moral, and religious education. She once gave her a beautiful book with paintings of major events in the Bible and would sit with her and explain them to her. Jeanette wore a beautiful white dress and little white pillbox hat on the occasion of her confirmation, and Gram gave Jeanette her first Bible. These two books became lifelong treasures.

Gram was the steady adult who gave her coins for the ice-cream truck that came around every day with its twinkling, familiar music. Sometimes old-fashioned, Gram was a constant reminder of stability, and Jeanette loved her.

It was at the end of the fourth grade when she was told that the next year she would be in a class for more advanced students. Jeanette had conflicting feelings about this change. On one hand, she was proud of it. On the other hand, it seemed scary. What if she couldn't do as well as the others? She had always seen herself as being, perhaps, the big fish in a little pond. This, however, could be the little fish in a big pond. It didn't match what she had imagined. She always felt uncomfortable during physical education; later she found out why.

Jeanette turned ten just before Christmas Eve in 1958, and the house was filled with the aromas of favorite foods. There was sledding, snow creatures, and Christmas lights. Josh was expecting a new bike, and Jeanette a huge stuffed animal tiger; she loved Christmas.

On this particular Christmas:

"Jeanette," called Gram. "Your dad is on the phone."

She was surprised since it was Christmas Eve, but she climbed in the big chair and took the phone from Gram.

"I wanted to tell you I won't be coming home," said Dad.

Jeanette couldn't say anything for a few seconds. "What? Why, Dad?"

"Your mom and I are getting a divorce."

Divorce? What does that mean?

Her stomach churned, and she felt the life energy seeping out of her body like an ocean wave retreating back into the sea. She began throwing up and sobbing unconsolably.

Her world was shattered—this was the worst Christmas.

Gram and Mom agreed that she and Josh should go to their aunt and uncle's house in the country.

Jeanette felt as though her life had ended. She and Josh stayed with her aunt and uncle and their two huge great Danes for over a week. She went for some walks in the woods by herself to explore and think. She heard the raccoons noisily getting into trashcans at night.

This was the first of many major traumatic events that would shape Jeanette as she learned to live with adversity and how to survive it.

She was finishing the fifth grade when Jeanette soon found herself in Miami, Florida, when her mom decided to remarry her former boss. He was being transferred, and they were to be married once they had moved, and Jeanette was to be a part of the wedding service.

It was strange to move that far away to a place she had barely heard anything about and basically start a new life. She had overheard extended family talk about the divorce and move. They talked about how her dad did not want to pay child support to her mom and hinted that the move to Miami and new marriage was Belle's way of getting around all the legal loopholes and start a new life. Apparently, she had to move to a southern state for three months to meet a requirement for getting a divorce at the time. This whole new *learning* for Jeanette contributed to a growing feeling of desertion by her dad.

This would transform into a fear of abandonment that would plague Jeanette for most of her life.

Miami was a whole different and exciting world for her—and for Josh. For the first time in her life, Jeanette was popular and admired for how well she did in school. She loved it and the possibility of dating and maybe even having a boyfriend.

She made a new best friend, another Pat, who lived at the end of their block. Sixth grade began in junior high; she was elected to positions and so enjoyed the new friendships.

Then—it happened again. Her stepdad was transferred now to Orlando, Florida, in the middle of the state. She didn't want to leave and cried when they loaded the car. Josh didn't want to leave and refused to go. He ended up staying with one of his friends. So, Jeanette was left alone without her protective brother by her side.

The house in Orlando was a step-up and literally at the

edge of an orange grove. The people were different, and Jeanette was not warmly embraced. She was treated as a total outsider. The air of superiority she felt from other girls her age was palpable, and she felt looked down on as their noses always seemed to be in the air.

She did manage to find two girlfriends to hang around with who apparently suffered from the same looked down upon persona. She had a boyfriend who was another outsider who rode a motorcycle. He was nearly killed in an accident and spent a whole year in the hospital or rehabilitation.

But then the birth of her little sister changed everything. Now she could just focus on this beautiful baby and taking care of her. At thirteen, Jeanette wanted to take over many of the responsibilities for her baby sister.

Then, her stepdad was transferred again, to Atlanta. But this time Jeanette couldn't wait to go.

Salvation!

They stayed in a motel for about two weeks until the new house was ready. Jeanette walked around the hotel grounds and sometimes went to Howard Johnsons for ice cream. One day she saw a handsome guy who looked to be about high school age standing near the playground.

His name was Jack, and his family was also staying temporarily at the hotel. He was to go to a high school not far from hers. They became immediate friends and soon began using the little playhouse at the playground as a place to kiss and then get an ice cream. They dated for a year and a half until Jack decided to join the navy. Jack was her first love and his kiss her first *real* kiss.

High school was boring, and there were a lot of cliques. She wanted to get on with her life, so she worked hard to graduate early and then started college at sixteen. She was eager to find her way in the future before her. She also knew that she would have to pay her own way, so right after being accepted at the university, she got a job in the admissions office where she would work through her undergraduate years. She loved her independence and enjoyed buying gifts for others. She got her stepdad a three-piece set of luggage for Christmas. He was a little embarrassed by it but accepted graciously. He was a good man.

Sages

Ellie scowled. "I just can't believe Robbie's father. It looks like his whole motivation in life was to make money, keep it for himself, and be admired by others, but certainly not by his family. They knew who he really was."

"You know *motivation* is a big deal," said Franklin. "If one looks at what drives a person, it can really tell you about whether to trust that person or not. It does require you to stop and think, be introspective, and get past the false personas people hide behind."

"Jeanette really loved her dad. Too bad she was estranged from him for a while. She felt abandoned, and this will be a sore spot throughout her life." Ellie sighed. "There are many kinds of abandonment, but in her case it was particularly hurtful as she misconstrued that her dad was rejecting her. In reality, he was still in love with his wife but hurt, and it was his way of protecting himself. Luckily, she did reconcile with her dad while living in Miami. She traveled by herself on trains, and at times, planes to visit him."

"One of the things that stands out about our two charges is their similar independence and self-responsibility," said Franklin. "You don't see that very often in people so young. Robbie was only seventeen when he left home after that horrific encounter with his father. He wasn't afraid to take a chance. Jeanette had that same level of independence and self-responsibility, starting college so young, taking responsibility for her life totally on her own."

"Robbie also showed *introspection* at an early age, and what a scary brush with death at that rayon factory." He knew he needed an education but had no idea how to pay for it. He could not and would not rely on his father for anything.

"You're so right, Ellie, these two young people were very mature for their ages. They didn't need to be told to do anything—they just did it."

The two sat in silent thought for several minutes.

Then Ellie said, "After being popular in Miami, Jeanette had to leave the place that had filled her with joy and a sense of accomplishment. That was really hard for her. It's funny that Josh refused to go—that took guts on his part. About a year later, he went out to Haight Asbury in California and became a hippie—the real deal. When Jeanette was just fifteen, he called her in Atlanta and asked if she could wire him some money. He had eaten nothing but peanut butter sandwiches for a month. So, Jeanette figured out how to do that on her own and sent him some money; he then went home to Atlanta, got his GED, and turned out he had the highest score ever. Then he applied and was accepted at Georgia Tech."

"Determined kids, all three of them," said Franklin. "Despite obstacles that got in their way. Jeanette showed a high degree of *empathy* which would characterize her the rest of her life, including an impact on her married life. She was a *rescuer* from back when she had her little animal clinic to her brother's rescue from hippie heaven."

Robbie

Robbie decided he was going to get a college education and find a way to pay for it himself. He started by getting a job and saving every penny toward his own college fund. Once Robbie had several thousand dollars, he had another idea. He wrote letters to twenty different small colleges asking if he could be a walk-on with their football team. He was good at baseball and had an interest in body building, but he had always loved football and had dreams of being a professional.

He got one reply.

Robbie was a walk-on for the football team at this State College. Unfortunately, walk-ons did not receive a scholarship, so his saved money only took him so far. Eventually, it ran out, and Robbie's only recourse was to ask his coach if there was any possible way he could get a scholarship. The coach must have recognized Robbie's potential not just as a player, but as a leader and found one for him. Determination again was a definite Robbie trait.

Another defining trait that influenced others, was his working out at the gym; repeatedly and strenuously. Pretty soon the others on the football team noticed what he was doing and decided to join him until almost all were following his lead and modeling his behavior. This leadership potential got Robbie elected to be captain of his college's football team at the end of his sophomore year and for the rest of his college career. This was a first; it had *never* happened before at this college. That honor usually went to seniors. Robbie was certainly admired for his dedication and persistence.

Robbie joined a fraternity, started dating, and found a girl he really liked. They were committed to one another, but she had to go away for the summer, and Robbie found himself in a relationship with another girl. His first love returned.

How can I be ready to get married when I did what I did this summer?

He confessed to her, and she was badly hurt.

Robbie felt terrible. This, and the previous emotional abuse from his father, led to the beginnings of an *almost* lifelong penchant toward self-criticism. It became part of his very being. Robbie didn't know who he really was.

He never wanted to hurt anyone. He remembered in school he was frequently getting into fights, but had an *epiphany*, which was one of Robbie's favorite words, every time this happened. He realized he was either breaking up a fight or helping the victim of bullies. That opened his eyes a little.

But self-criticism was—the ruler of Robbie—until it wasn't.

Robbie didn't make it to the NFL, but in his work after college graduation, he was making more money than he had ever imagined. Something didn't quite fit though—he didn't love what he was doing. He continued his body building, but he didn't have passion for a job or profession.

One day a friend of his called from Atlanta, Georgia, and asked him to come south and be one of the football coaches at the high school he was working at. Robbie hesitated, considering the good money he was making, but within minutes made up his mind.

Why not?

He later told his friend, "I'm on my way."

This was a totally different environment for Robbie. Atlanta was huge; it was astounding to him.

Football coaches at that time were required to teach an academic class or two along with their coaching duties. And, almost laughably, he was assigned to teach Georgia History.

I can't even find my way home from school, and they want me to teach a subject that I know nothing about.

Robbie walked into the classroom with the students in front of him. With his characteristic humor, he totally relaxed everyone. Robbie fell in love—with teaching. He later taught science—his other great love but always saw himself as a *teacher* no matter what role he was in.

Robbie loved teaching and coaching young football players, other athletes, and designing the best training for them, and for himself. Because Robbie was a *walk the walk* person, he was dedicated to being the best he could be. However, a lot depended on who one worked with in the educational environment.

Although many were supportive and enthusiastic about his ideas, one was downright nasty. After Robbie had done an exhaustive study of needs to improve both the training and safety of athletes, his head coach said to him, "I don't care about any of that! We're winning football games!"

Robbie was taken aback but also incensed at the lack of regard for the very students they were supposed to be taking care of. The head coach snapped, "We seem to have a difference of opinion. I don't think we will be able to work together anymore."

"I don't think so either," said Robbie. "I quit."

Robbie had principles and values and would stick up for them despite the consequences. Actually, it turned out to be a good move. As word got out, two other schools in the district quickly tried to recruit Robbie to come to their respective schools. For the first time, Robbie felt he had some leverage. He decided to go for it and submitted his requirements.

Robbie told them he would only come if he could train every single athlete in the school, rather a large group of students. He said he wanted to teach and train them for all six sessions of the day, forgoing a period off. Every athlete had to take his class—no exceptions. It was his dream, and he got it. The next years were a testament to his passion, and results for the students were phenomenal. Robbie was in his element.

As his educational career continued, Robbie began to realize that he needed to pursue more advanced degrees, not only to make more money, but to really make a difference and have more authority to do things better. So, he began attending a university, although he had to travel several hours after school to attend classes to get both his master's degree and Specialist Degree in Educational Administration. Robbie really wanted to get a PhD, but this university did not offer one in his field.

Here was a man guided by his own strong desire to make a difference and to help others. It was fundamental to his life.

Jeanette

JEANETTE LOVED the atmosphere at college. She was in her element; mingling with so many people, the vastness of the courses, and interests they invoked within her. She had a lot of required courses to take her first year, but she started out in geology. Her least favorite course was math; it always had been. So, she looked for an alternative that would count for math credit. She enrolled in a junior level philosophy course in logic, and she loved it. She particularly liked the detective aspect of it, and the satisfaction when she correctly solved a proof. She earned an A+, back when they gave pluses in school.

Jeanette was still classified as majoring in geology, but when she started courses in other areas, her interest in that subject began to wane. There was so much wonderfulness to learn. Jeanette's brother had come over to her university now and was doing well. His mind was particularly adept at computer science, a brand-new happening that made him a unique asset. One day the head geology professor walked into the admissions office, and when Jeanette looked up, he said, "You are so good at what you do. You need to be sure to keep going for graduate school in geology."

She was thrilled but shy about taking compliments. She didn't realize that her brother had stepped into the room out of her view. She said, "Thank you."

The professor said, "I'm not talking about you. I'm talking about him." He pointed to her brother. Then he added, "You're not smart enough to do that."

Jeanette felt as if she had been stabbed with a knife. The one thing she hated the most in people was arrogance, and this guy was full of it—without an ounce of empathy. She decided then and there that geology was off the table. Besides she had been taking classes in Geography and Psychology and loved them. She would much prefer to work with understanding people in different countries, learning about things like continental drift and the makings of the mind in people than studying rocks anyway. This was her first experience with misogyny, although at this time, girls could wear only dresses to school, not pants. How ridiculous.

In her senior year, Jeanette took a course in Psychological Assessment and was hooked. She now knew exactly what she wanted to do and began her initial graduate school plans.

Jeanette decided to join a sorority. All the sororities and fraternities had large rooms taking up the entire second floor of the Student Center. Since this was an urban university, they could not have the large houses that characterized most other colleges. Jeanette chose a sorority that seemed more involved with good work, real friendships, and learning. Not the glamour and partying of other sororities. She enjoyed it and felt it added a lot to her college experience. She was named Vice President of Scholarship to help others keep their grades high.

Most of the sisters in her sorority ended up dating guys from the fraternities. Jeanette did this, too, although not as much as others. The biggest thing that could happen to a sister was to get pinned by a fellow from a fraternity. Jeanette watched this happen time after time. When it did, they held a secret ceremony in the big room. All the lights were turned out, and the sisters formed a circle. A single candle was slowly passed from girl to girl. When the candle reached the pinned girl, she would blow it out, the lights would go on, and everyone would cheer and celebrate her.

Jeanette wanted this so badly. It finally did happen, but it would be ironic that, in later years, she would not remember the name of this young man. She did remember being excited to have the ceremony in her honor.

There is one name Jeanette would *never* forget. This would be one of the first tragedies she would face in her life. She dated a boy from one of the fraternities. They liked each other a lot; Jeanette was seventeen and a sophomore. She remembered the smell of his aftershave and his tender eyes. He was a junior and decided to join the navy. Jeanette continued her schoolwork, her promotion in the admissions office, and activities in the sorority.

They had made no commitments.

Jeanette was still living at home. One day her mother called her at work to tell her that two dozen red roses had just arrived for her. Her mom read her the card; they were from her former boyfriend in the navy. Mom was impressed. She let her feelings known when she was impressed but refrained from saying anything when she wasn't.

About thirty minutes later, he and a friend showed up at her office. He was on leave and wanted to take her out that evening. They went to a park; it was fall, and the slight smell of campfire smoke and coolness permeated the air. He pulled her into his arms, kissed her, and told her how much he had missed her. It was clear that he wanted to get engaged before he went back to base. He took her home and said he would come back the next day.

This had come as a complete surprise to Jeanette, and she pondered it all night. She wasn't sure she was in love with him. She had her own dreams and future. He showed her a family ruby ring, and she struggled but made her decision.

The next day he came, along with his friend. She had expected him to be alone; this was awkward. She explained she was so young and didn't want to make a commitment. The look on his face was devastating to Jeanette. She clearly hurt him, and she didn't like to hurt anyone; that wasn't her intention. They left, and Jeanette went home and talked to her mom.

Two days later there was a news report that two intoxicated young navy men were hit by a train and killed. Jeanette's heart almost stopped, and she was overwhelmed with guilt. She felt she had *caused* their deaths by her actions. It was too much to bear. She went home to cry and talk with her mother. Mom decided that they would go to the funeral together. She thought it would help Jeanette, and it did.

He was buried in a beautiful cemetery with a lake and swans where her mom and stepdad would later be buried. Jeanette visited his grave a few times, but it was far. This time Jeanette resisted being a *rescuer*, and in her mind, this was the result.

This was the second of the tragedies Jeanette would face, but it wouldn't be the last.

Sages

"Their similarities are amazing," said Ellie. "I mean, Jeanette and Robbie. It is obvious that they share so many qualities and beliefs. What do you think, Franklin?"

Franklin nodded. "I see it too. I'm blown away by their independence. Both were on their own at a young age. They're both responsible, like taking it upon themselves to finance their educations, not ever asking for help, even from parents."

"You know, Franklin, Robbie has a lot to overcome because of the way his father treated him." She sighed. "Always disparaging him, never appreciating him, never giving any indication at all that he loved him, only seeing him as an appendage who was just expected to do as he was told. He hated his father—but he wasn't afraid of him. Robbie's brave; and so is Jeanette."

"Thank God." He glanced up. "Sorry, Boss…for his loving mother. Robbie will learn a lot about her at her funeral. One thing, year after year she volunteered at the prison every

Friday. She never sought recognition, even from her family. She was a remarkable woman."

"I think Robbie inherited his kindness from his mother," said Ellie. "We've seen enough to know having even one positive person in your life, can keep a child from repeating the negative characteristics of a parent."

"Jeanette will face a lot of tragedies. She already suffers from feelings of abandonment, anxiety, and fears that started in childhood. Then after the death of her former boyfriend, her guilt is too much. I think—and I bet you do too, Ellie, that the two will need to have a lot of strength."

"Some experiences change who we are fundamentally. Each one has the potential to be powerful and can be a positive or negative influence. The key word is *choice.* Most people on Earth don't realize this. You know how we're always taught; *it's your choice.* Our choices either build or diminish the soul, and Jeanette is a big-time rescuer. I wonder if that is going to cause her problems in the future. Remember, when she didn't rescue her navy boyfriend, he ended up dying. That's a heavy load."

"It really is. That's another trait they share. They set goals and persist until they reach them. That is going to help them throughout their lives." Franklin smiled. "They'll have experiences on Earth to find out what love is—and more importantly—what it isn't. It won't be easy."

Ellie sighed. "It will be interesting to see how they manage that—if they do."

Robbie

ROBBIE WAS A BORN TEACHER; he loved learning new things and passing on that knowledge to others. He had many different roles during his thirty years in education, but he had his favorites.

Once he got to design his own curriculum and taught every athlete in the school for six periods a day. That was definitely one of them. And it had only happened after he had that altercation with the head coach where what Robbie saw from him was arrogance and total lack of empathy. He quit, and it was a good thing when—because of that—he got exactly what he wanted at another school.

When Robbie was given *autonomy*, he really shined. During his career, he helped several football students eventually play in the Super Bowl. The girls track team went from being last place to winning the State Championship. This happened frequently. He was good, but never boastful. Robbie just did good work, respected his charges, and took his joy from their success. Robbie believed in the way he did things but knew he could always be better.

He researched and studied continuously, a *lifelong learner;* always looking for a better way of doing things. He loved science. Robbie had to know the *why* of everything. In his younger days, he would say he did it the wrong way. He followed a regimen that would build up the body so one would be as muscular as possible; at the same time tearing down joints by the excessive wear and tear.

His shoulder and knee replacements were a testament to that. Robbie had no hesitation in admitting he was wrong. This characteristic continued throughout his life, and he respected that quality in others.

Robbie's favorite job was as a high school principal at a school that was known as *gang central.* Probably the most challenging position any principal could have. It was the one high school he hoped he didn't get. Robbie had about a month on campus before the old principal retired, giving him time to become acclimated. He formed his own philosophy of what the school needed to be and what he wanted it to be like.

The teachers didn't know what to expect from this young-looking physically fit man; they waited nervously. He walked up to the microphone and said, "I'm going to say something that will sound very different to you." He lowered his voice to a whisper. "I don't care about SAT scores."

You could hear a pin drop. The teachers looked at him

with unbelieving eyes as he continued, "That's not our objective here. Our objective is to create knowledgeable and productive citizens. That's it."

Later, Robbie talked about expectations. He said, "I will be in the classrooms very frequently." He expected every teacher to know each student's first name and to use it. "If you don't," he said, "it's obvious that there is something wrong, and you have not bought into the objective here. We will talk, and if things do not get better, I will love you right out of the building."

Since Robbie was a *walk the walk* person, every class change, he would be in the hallways and would greet each student by name if he knew it. If not, he would say, "Hi, I'm Mr. Walker. I'm good at remembering faces, but names sometimes get me. Tell me yours again." He'd repeat it and say, "Glad to see you, Jeremiah." By the end of the year, only five months away, he would know the names of one thousand students in this big high school of about twenty-five hundred.

A *gang-central* school was especially challenging. He had an innovative way of addressing issues. At lunch, he would find a table in the cafeteria with known gang members and sit right in the middle of them. The first time he did this the kids were in disbelief. Gradually, they opened up and even joked with him. Then he'd be on to another table to do the same thing.

It did pay off. One of those gang members became his undercover informant. One day he told Robbie about a big fight that was set to take place behind the school that afternoon. These rival gangs numbered about a hundred students. There was every possibility that there would be numerous hurt or even killed. Since Robbie had been alerted, he suggested the police to be there in force at the designated time. When they did, the gang members just disappeared. Although Robbie enjoyed making such a difference at this school for the five years he was there, it was a highly stressful job.

Stress really flared one day when there was a bomb threat at the school. Robbie called the police, and they did a sweep, found what looked like an active bomb, and told him to get everybody out of there. They evacuated all twenty-five hundred students and staff and set up places for them to go within walking distance of the school.

A second police specialist group had checked the bomb and felt it was real. Robbie told teachers to lock their doors in case there were valuables in the room.

In the middle of everything, Robbie's mom called, "Robbie are you alright? You're on CNN with all this bomb stuff at your school."

His response was quick. "I'm fine, Mom, but a little busy right now. Call you later."

Hours later, the police determined that the bomb was not active, and everyone could go home. However, the teachers had locked their doors and wouldn't be able to get their car keys. Another dilemma. Robbie located the one person he knew would have access to all the keys, a member of the janitorial staff, and they systematically went to each of the many classroom doors to open them. What a day! Without a doubt this was one of Robbie's most stressful days, but it was also his favorite job ever.

Robbie really made a difference at that high school. He exuded a combination of innovation and kind authority that won over almost all of the teachers. Yes, there were a few he had to love out of the building, but there were many that thought the world of him—teachers, staff, and students.

At one point in his career, Robbie and another administrator were given the job of flying to the Philippines to recruit teachers as this school system had a notable lack of qualified teachers. They both did this with enthusiasm. If anyone could be successful, it would be these two; and they were. Eighteen well-qualified teachers had signed contracts. Many sold their houses, furniture, and made travel arrangements to come to the United States.

However, the new female superintendent was enamored with her own sense of power. After the two successful recruiters brought back their signed contracts—exactly what their mission was—she decided that she didn't want them. Robbie literally could not believe it. So, he met with her accompanied by the personnel head. She was so arrogant, uncaring, incredibly dismissive, and rude. The teachers had already made sacrifices. He was extremely frustrated, and sad. He had let those teachers down.

He lost it and demanded, "How can you do that?"

The personnel head had to pull him back to get him out of there.

After that, the power-obsessed superintendent did not forget Robbie. In a short time, he was told he would no longer be the principal at his beloved high school; she created a position in the athletic department for him to *transfer to*. He could have retired with full benefits but decided to stay on. So, he also addressed that position with innovation and excellent work, much to the chagrin of Superintendent Power Lady. But she kept up her vengeance by telling him he would now have to be a teacher. Robbie loved teaching, but due to his pension, he decided to retire.

Ironically, Power Lady was soon out of there, fired by the board.

Robbie's retirement lasted three days. He couldn't stand it. He began a new career using his teaching skills, exercise science, and mostly, his desire to help people.

Jeanette

After receiving her master's degree in school psychology, Jeanette needed to find a job in her field. She had always had jobs but this was different—this was her career. She wanted to stay in the same geographical area, so she set her sights on a medium-sized school system south of where she was living. After doing some research, she learned that this school district contracted out for psychological services through a large cooperative agency.

Jeanette wanted to start an entire Psychological Services Division from the ground up. She didn't want to be just another cog in the wheel; she wanted to innovate and develop. So, she found out who was responsible for hiring and made an appointment.

She asked, "Have you ever thought about having your own psychologist for your school system rather than doing everything through the cooperative?"

He paused for a minute then said, "No, I haven't, but I would like to know more about why that could benefit us."

Jeanette launched into her proposal, and an hour later, she was hired as the first psychologist they had ever had. She was thrilled. It meant that she could design exactly what a Psychological Services Department should be all about and build it from scratch. Keeping to a model of excellence, innovation, research, and maintaining the highest quality for all services would be fundamental for her.

The department quickly grew by leaps and bounds. The school system rapidly recognized the benefit of having their own psychologists. Jeanette began designing the entire range of services they would provide. Some school systems only used psychologists for *testing* because that was required by law. But it required a new mindset, and Jeanette would find herself having to fight for the integrity of what she believed in for her department. Old habits are sometimes hard to break, but quality and excellence cannot be denied.

Under her program, when psychologists on her staff did psychological evaluations of students, they were required to thoroughly explore the student's strengths and weaknesses, arrive at a diagnosis, and then design—in detail—an appropriate way for the student to learn effectively, to control emotional or behavioral difficulties, and to achieve. It required a wealth of knowledge, and her psychologists were expected to continuously keep learning and innovating. Jeanette wanted evaluations coming from her department to be better than expensive ones from psychologists in private practice, thoroughly exploring all the students' needs.

Jeanette's psychologists were researchers as well and developed training workshops for teachers on the most pertinent methods for teaching all students, and innovative courses on the brain and how it works. They provided consistent, high-quality training for teachers and administrators on a variety of subjects that greatly improved teaching and learning for all students. The department engaged in their own research and then developed programs based on that research to be implemented in many schools throughout the system, and eventually in many school systems within the State.

No one else was doing this. The results of this implementation and formal research model gained national attention. Jeanette and selected psychologists from her staff trained numerous schools throughout the state in this proven and easily replicated program at almost no cost to school systems. Presentations were requested everywhere. The National School Boards Association loved it. So did many other national groups. It brought much positive attention to this little school system on a national and state level.

Jeanette loved training psychologists to do extraordinary work. She never let her standards and expectations slide. At one time she had four PhD's on her staff; to have even one would be quite a rarity in the state. Psychologists wanted to work there because it was everything they dreamed they could be. Jeanette also recruited interns from universities;

some were compensated and some were not. She soon was called upon to develop other major initiatives for the school system, such as the System School Safety Plan after the first mass shooting at a school (Columbine High) changed the world of education.

She wrote research grants for schools and designated psychologists did as well. Suffice to say, Jeanette and her Psychological Services Department won every award and honor possible in the state.

Jeanette also headed up major state-level committees for the State Department of Education on various topics and needs. It was rewarding to her to make a difference and help so many people in so many ways. She felt it was her calling; there was so much to do. She served on the *cabinet* for the school superintendent where needs and possible interventions could be discussed. It was a lot, but it too was rewarding.

And then it was not.

A new female assistant school superintendent was hired to focus mostly on curriculum and on the *power* chart , she became Jeanette's immediate supervisor and was very difficult to deal with. She kept making ridiculous demands of Jeanette, such as, "I want you to turn around these three schools."

Jeanette pondered, *What in the world does that mean? What criteria would be used to determine this?*

The lady assistant superintendent had no clue. Her unreasonable demands made Jeanette's position impossible.

By this time Jeanette already had her PhD in neuropsychology and her dissertation had won the Outstanding

Dissertation Award at her university. She had also passed the National Exam required for Psychological Private Practice and was contemplating leaving the school system and going into full-time private practice. She had worked in the school system for twenty-five years and had been doing some part-time private practice as well.

She needed five more years to get a full pension from the state. She remembered she had worked at one of the State Universities when she was sixteen. She contacted them, and they agreed to have one of their staff go and search the vault for her records.

Success!

She found five years of work credit, at a ridiculously low pay wage—but that didn't matter, it still counted.

Jeanette sent the girl who did the work a huge bouquet of flowers to thank her.

The new lady assistant superintendent was relentless. What motivated her to behave this way? It had to be power-grabbing, and her desire to be a school superintendent someday. Jeanette's autonomy was now threatened. The lady assistant superintendent partnered with a couple of other administrators to call for an audit of psychological services with the goal of reducing their role back twenty-five years to a limited role. They were supposed to provide an oral presentation of their findings.

Jeanette flat refused to go. It was all a sham, and an obvious sham as well.

Then a very funny thing happened. The superintendent

appeared at Jeanette's office door, huffing and puffing. He was mad; he paced back and forth in front of her desk admonishing her for not attending the presentation and wanted her to get over there. His face was red as he grumbled while Jeanette sat calmly at her desk, watching him.

He said, "This borders on insubordination!"

All Jeanette had to hear was the word *borders* to know she had the upper hand. She very calmly said to him, "Jimmy, please sit down. You're going to have a heart attack."

She serenely stated her point of view and feelings that this was all a setup due to a couple of people's desire for power and lack of managerial skills.

"You need to get over there." He finally left.

He exited for the stairs that led back to his office, and she could hear him huff and puff like the wolf in the three little pigs.

On the way he met up with another psychologist, Connie, and began to lament to her how Jeanette was difficult to deal with.

He told her, "I just sent Barbara down to Macon to learn how to evaluate school psychologists and here Jeanette is refusing to do something that Barbara arranged."

Connie said quietly, but forcibly, "Do you know who developed the State evaluation system for school psychologists?"

Jimmy responded, "No."

"Jeanette did."

His face could have won a photo contest for the expression of complete resignation.

The proverbial straw occurred the following week when the yearly evaluation reports for all staff came out. An evaluation was completed by the assistant lady superintendent. For the first time in her life, Jeanette received an NI or needs improvement.

Jeanette had not turned around the three schools yet, that she was asked to do four months earlier, and she had not completed as many evaluations as other psychologists.

What!?

Assistant Lady seemed to have forgotten that Jeanette was the Director of Psychological Services and had more on her plate than any other administrator there. It was so absurd, it was laughable. She wrote a four-page letter to her *supervisor*, the superintendent and the members of the Board of Education directly attacking the veracity of the NI.

Jeanette decided then and there that she was leaving at the end of the school year, just a month away. At this time there were five full-time school psychologists on staff. All but one of these psychologists, the cream of the crop in the State, left with her.

The excellence left with them just as Jeanette knew it would. You need to fight for what you believe is right, and you must make decisions that reflect your values, beliefs, and core principles. Jeanette had loved this time in this public school system. She made sure that the poorest of the poor received the same level of services as the well-off, and each benefitted by the highest quality they could receive publicly or privately.

The assistant lady superintendent didn't last very long. She didn't get the position she tried for, she did get another one for a short period of time in a small county, but she soon left.

For Jeanette, the time was right for a full-time private practice.

She spent eighteen more years in the profession with a full-time private practice in neuropsychology, specializing in children and adolescents. Her childhood desire to do something in life like *Marcus Welby, MD*, was fulfilled.

She built a full practice on the lower level of her home. She had a large office, back office, waiting room, educational assistant's office, and a bathroom with a separate entrance. She hired a secretary/office manager and began getting referrals from doctors, neurologists, schools, and parents.

It was what she always wanted. Total autonomy to do what she knew was best and for the joy of figuring out what was going on in a student's brain. She could thoroughly assess a student's strengths and challenges, and design exactly what each needed to help them be successful. Jeanette's schedule was always full simply from word of mouth; she never had to advertise. She had a wonderful reputation because she gave her all to every family and her reports were well received by parents and professionals alike.

At the same time, Jeanette served as the consulting neuropsychologist for a prestigious private school in Atlanta, spending eight years there. After that, she was recruited to help build the curriculum and ways of improving the education for young students with at least two disabilities such as autism, learning disabilities, emotional and behavioral problems, and/or neurological problems. As before, she started from scratch; training the wonderful teachers there.

Jeanette knew by the time she retired that she had probably had one of the best careers, if not the best, that any person could ever have. She received such satisfaction from figuring things out, consulting with other professionals, designing, and creating effective ways to help others. The latter was a major emphasis in her life. She always wanted to help people. Parents were so grateful; for the first time they understood what was happening with their kid. And they knew exactly what to do about it. There is nothing better than that to please one's soul.

In the realm of the profession, life was very good for Jeanette. However, in other realms, despair and tragedy, not so much.

How much could one person bear?

Sages

"THE SIMILARITIES between these two just keep on coming. Both of them loved being teachers, and they were both phenomenal in their jobs," said Ellie. "Robbie was a teacher as we usually think of it, but even when he became a principal, he was still teaching. He taught about a new way of thinking about their purpose and taught about treating others with respect and the value of kind authority. And he modeled this every day himself."

"Jeanette loved teaching teachers and parents so they could learn to understand their children and how to help them. She even loved teaching administrators so they could understand things a little better and use the information available to them in a more productive way. Jeanette also constantly taught the many interns and later all those postdoctoral students she supervised.

"They were both teachers at heart," said Franklin. "Teaching in various forms was the steady, essential component of their professional lives."

"You know, Franklin, they could only do this because they were both lifelong learners. Neither one was ever comfortable with a static set of knowledge. They both had to learn more; they were always seeking new knowledge and better ways to help people," said Ellie.

"I'm not sure they realize this yet," said Franklin. "But I think they both at least unconsciously know their purpose in life. And what is amazing is they both have the same purpose, to help others. Another thing, they both need *autonomy*. It is essential to them to do their best work. They both thought differently from others and wanted to put their visions into action. That's why autonomy was so important."

"That's true, and another thing they both *stick to their principles*. They had certain values, standards, and principles they lived by. When things were against their core values, they challenged authority, especially if they knew they were right. I loved when Robbie just quit when that head coach basically said he didn't care about the athletes, that he just wanted to win games."

Ellie laughed. "Franklin, I love the way you are beginning to express yourself! You go, tiger!"

Franklin chuckled and rolled his eyes. "Then the new Superintendent Power Lady, full of arrogance and lacking in any semblance of empathy. She took him away from the school he loved. She was so into her own authority that she couldn't even see she was shooting herself in the foot."

Ellie scoffed. "Superintendent Power Lady only had to look in the mirror to see what ugliness and lack of compassion looks like. Aren't you glad we got to be flies on the wall to see Jeanette and Jimmy having it out in her office. That was hysterical! Watching Jimmy pacing back and forth, red-faced while Jeanette leaned back serene in her chair. And then she told him to have a seat before he had a heart attack. That was priceless! I love seeing people stand up to ridiculousness and stand by their principles."

"I really learned something today—the power of examining a person's motivation for doing something. We would all be better if we did this more. Sometimes it only takes a few minutes of thinking and introspection to accomplish this." Franklin thought for a minute. "Take Robbie's Superintendent Power Lady. Her motivation in doing what she did to Robbie and all those recruited teachers from the Philippines was to save face and prove her power as the new superintendent. It was totally self-centered. And Superintendent Jimmy's rant with Jeanette was to show authority or thought he would lose the respect of a couple of his administrators. Jeanette knew this when it was happening. She also knew Jimmy well and could pick up that he really didn't like what he was doing."

"Anytime you see the combination of desire for power over others and selfishness, that motivation is a very bad one," said Ellie. "Neither Robbie nor Jeanette ever showed that. What a similarity."

Robbie

Now that Robbie had retired from his career in education, he began a new career utilizing many of the skills he had learned over the years. It would be difficult to find a *correct* name for what Robbie did. Some people might call him a *trainer,* an *exercise coach,* a *physical fitness instructor,* or some other name conjuring up a fit guy in a gym instructing others how to get in better shape.

But that was not Robbie.

He was very different from other instructors in a gym who put people on machines and tell them how many minutes to stay there.

No, Robbie was very different. First, he believed that his clients, who he insisted on calling friends, needed to understand the *why* of what they were doing. He was an expert on the science of the human body and how to make it function better. His goal wasn't to make a friend/client have big muscles that would impress the world, but to function to their maximum extent possible for their own health and well-being. Robbie admitted that he totally changed his perspective from his youth after his own research and learning took him in an entirely different direction. In his mind, if you couldn't explain why a particular exercise would benefit the unique needs of Client A, you would not be really helping that person. That would be a game changer in this profession.

Robbie knew that in order to do that, you must first assess to know exactly where a person is to begin with. Then listen carefully and evaluate what their goal is. Then, design every exercise that would allow that person to reach their own personal goals.

As he advanced in age, he found that his clients and friends were also getting older. Many had injuries, physically handicapping conditions, and obstacles that could prevent them from active participation in daily life. This change in the served population was gradual, but by his late sixties, he was working mainly with people older than him, some into their nineties. However, Robbie went through a period where he was dramatically overworking himself.

In Robbie's mind, a primary goal was to help others. He didn't like to turn anyone down, sometimes seeing people for no charge, because he knew he could help them. That need to help others he eventually regarded as his prime purpose in life. So, with that mindset, he set himself up to be overworked seeing massive numbers of clients each day. However, Robbie was happiest when he was in that gym atmosphere working with his people. He was not a social animal, but no one there would ever know that. He was so dedicated to each and every client and their progress; it always became very personal to him.

After assessing and determining what was most important to his clients, Robbie insisted on a tangible assessment of their progress. He kept meticulous records on each client so he could demonstrate improvement with the quality of a science experiment. Robbie and some of his most devoted clients became their own Lab Rats to test out hypotheses and the value of what they were putting into place. It was much like the *by-in* he required of his teachers at the high school where he was principal. Previously and with a different mindset, he had relied on learned exercises from others and the use of machines. Now he was creating exercises for individuals to build functionality, muscle, stability, and strength so that people of older ages could live life in the best way possible. He didn't use machines for them much in the gym, just occasionally, but relied on his own knowledge and skills to create individualized programs for them. It was marvelous to watch.

Not only was Robbie a skilled exercise scientist, but one of the kindest people to his clients. He genuinely cared about each one. That was why he insisted upon calling them friends; most of them became just that after spending time with him. In this atmosphere, Robbie was cheerful, usually had a smile on his face, and loved a silly joke. Robbie stood out; he was different from other *trainers*. He was fully invested, so attentive, had incredible knowledge, and was always helpful, kind, and caring.

Robbie was also doing things to help people outside of this exercise science realm. In 1999, he was called upon to go to Hanoi in North Vietnam as a part of what is best described as an *undercover* mission trip. At this time, missionaries were only allowed into North Vietnam if there was a secular, helpful to North Vietnam reason for their trip. There was a Christian missionary couple from the United States living there and offered services setting up a physical training program and gym at the Hanoi Agricultural University. This was also in conjunction with the Disabled Sports Federation of that country. Robbie was also told that Hanoi was looking for an expert from the United States to help with their country's training for the Olympics.

Robbie was asked to try to find someone willing to go there but had no luck. It sounded interesting, so he decided to go himself. The area they had set aside to be the gym was little more than a hallway randomly filled with old, primitive equipment. The heat was stifling. Robbie gave advice about setting up the gym and doing training. While there, he was deeply affected by the poverty he saw all around him. He had a picture of homeless children, who seemed to be starving, sitting on the floor in a cluttered room making beautiful carvings that could be sold for a small amount to help pay for their upkeep. A kind man had taken them in to his workshop so they would have a place to stay. The floor was dusty, and the boys and girls were working hard to learn how to carve their beautiful figurines.

Robbie and the others on the trip were housed at the elegant five-star Daewoo Hotel, with a huge lobby, which was the size of several houses. It was graced with unusual pools and palm trees. The contrast between this hotel and the actual place they wanted to go to undercover was beyond striking. They were headed to a tiny village called Mai Chau, where true missionary work had been going on.

On the way, they had the scare of a lifetime. As they were pulling up to an area, they suddenly found themselves surrounded by North Vietnamese Army men who pointed their rifles directly at the heads of those in the vehicle. All of the group that had come from the United States, including the couple leading the missionary work there, were in that vehicle. Robbie was in the back seat. Directly in front of him was the young black-haired Vietnamese pastor who had done such great work in Mai Chau to help people learn about the meanings of true Christianity. Guns were pointed at every head except this pastor. He was one of the most wanted people in the country, but it was like they didn't see him. This was truly amazing to Robbie; how could they not see him. After a time, they let them go on. They were back on their way to Mai Chau.

Once there, they were invited to spend the night in a house and sat on the floor with refreshments while the wanted Vietnamese pastor began speaking to the owners of this house. The place where they lived was referred to as New Hope Valley. It was so hot there and extremely dark outside.

Robbie's visit to Mai Chau was life-changing for him. Although these people had to work hard, getting up at dawn to work in the rice fields and finishing only when it got dark, they were happy and cheerful. The young boys and girls seemed to be dressed in their finest for their visitors and were so fascinated to see their own pictures on a cell phone. They looked just like American children; happy and intrigued with a new toy and seeing their own reflections in a picture. They were beautiful—in every way. The village invited the group in for tea in the afternoons. They sat in a circle on the floor around the food mat. They ate what were likely lavish dinners with nine or ten bowls from which all took their helpings. Robbie, who had always been super sensitive to spicy anything, was always careful. The kids loved the soccer ball their guests had brought for them.

They visited several houses during their stay in Mai Chau. On their last night at about 9:00 p.m., there was a celebration with young girl dancers all dressed alike in pale blue tops, long dark blue skirts, and multicolored bands around their middle and white headbands. The church in New Hope Valley quadrupled that night. A hard day in the rice fields would begin the next day at 5:30 a.m. Or perhaps spinning thread using an old bicycle wheel. The only fresh water in the village came from a small, narrow waterfall graced on each side with thick, green foliage. The villagers bathed and washed clothes in this small stream.

After living in the United States, Robbie realized we take so much for granted. His desire for helping people quadrupled that night.

Before leaving for home, Robbie went to see the changing of the guard at the Ho Chi Minh Mausoleum in Hanoi. There was no way to get close to the Presidential Palace as it was guarded vigorously. A particularly odious place for him was the street markets where bowl after bowl of fish, meats, tongues, livers, and brains laid out for hours in the stifling heat. The fruits and vegetables market, though, was very colorful and overseen by women who had helped to produce them.

Robbie managed to visit wrestlers drilling at the #1 National Sports Training Center in Hanoi. He again saw Professor Giang who was the Secretary General of the North Vietnamese Olympic Team and Head of the Hanoi Sports Department. Since Robbie had been unable to find any qualified candidate to advise about training for their Olympic Team, he was introduced to them as the *expert* on sports training from the United States.

He had decided to go one other place before he left Hanoi. He waited until the end, deliberately. Cameras were not allowed inside this place, but he has a picture of himself on the outside at the guard tower. Whenever Robbie talks about this place, which is hard for him to do, it overwhelms him. When he went inside, he was overcome by the presence of pure evil. This is the Hanoi Hilton, where American soldiers such as John McCain were housed. It was stark; unending concrete walls and floors with no light, no amenities at all. The floor of each cell was sloped toward one end. There were no toilets, rather a prisoner had to go near the slope and do his business. All the urine and excrement would eventually just go down the slope where it would stay. No water, no anything in this ghastly place. Robbie was devastated and felt physically sick imagining people stuck in this hellhole for long periods of time.

Robbie was not finished with this kind of helping people in his life. The couple who had lived in North Vietnam while they did their ministry were soon told that they had three days to get out of the country or they would be put in jail. They left and re-established their work in Thailand. Robbie made twelve trips there, teaching English as a second language to kids and adults, and he taught teachers how to do a better job. He loved every minute of it. But one of the things he really loved was getting great massages that cost hardly anything. Like the leader he is, he soon had the whole group going to get these fantastic massages while also supporting the people who made their living in this way.

Robbie was eventually put in charge of the program which included recruiting other people to join them and design the actual work they would do. He was on the board of directors which was housed at Georgia Tech for many years.

This work was at the core of who Robbie really is. He gets

such gratification from helping people. To see their smiles, their successes, their excitement when they have accomplished something they didn't think they could do, and to be part of their joy. It is like lifeblood for him.

Jeanette

JEANETTE WAS TWENTY-FIVE YEARS OLD when the unthinkable happened. Her forty-nine-year-old vivacious, universally adored mom Belle was diagnosed with breast cancer. It was hard for her when Jeanette automatically seemed to switch roles with her. She felt like her mom's mother and understood her need to be taken care of emotionally. At this time, Jeanette was living with her then husband, attending graduate school at the same time, and working full time in the school system. Jeanette lived on the other side of Atlanta, roughly an hour away. Thankfully, her beloved grandmother was available to come down and be with her daughter.

There was hope since Belle was being treated at Emory University, the premier university hospital at that time. However, things really didn't get better. Within a year, the cancer had spread to her brain, and hope faded away. It was hard seeing her own mother, always a vital part of her life, slip away into an almost unrecognizable person. Belle tried so hard to smile and show enjoyment with the last family trip she attended to their beloved St. Simons Island, but everyone knew Belle had lost the spark that had dazzled so many during her life.

Jeanette and her husband raised basset hounds, and one day Jeanette brought up ten little puppies and put them all on Belle's bed. Who could resist the joy in the most adorable, soft puppies all over you. It did help. There were sparks of smiles and laughter as these cuddly creatures romped all over Jeanette's mom.

Jeanette tried to get up to see her mom as often as she could. Her Gram would fill her in on how things were going, and one day told her it was getting close, and she should come. So, Jeanette went with her husband and found Belle slipping in and out of consciousness. She was surrounded by her family members, including their next-door neighbors who were as close as family. Suddenly her mom began talking to family members that were not there, who had already died. It was amazing to watch. After several hours, Jeanette and her husband decided, since it was getting late, they should leave and come back the next day.

Ironically, Jeanette was taking a course on Death and Dying at her university. She became fascinated by the brand-new revelations of near-death experiences which were first written about that very year in Dr. Raymond Moody's profound book, *Life After Life*. Thus began a lifelong knowledge quest to study more and more about these experiences as they became readily recognized and accepted. This *learning* substantially helped to form Jeanette's spiritual self.

When she arrived home after leaving her mom's, the phone was ringing. She was told her mother had passed away. At that moment with her ear on the receiver, Jeanette felt a wave that she still has difficulty describing that started at her head and moved down through her feet. She sank to the floor. It was a wave of such despair and loss; as if her mom was silently but definitely leaving her. Simultaneously, it was a wave of understanding that she would not have her mom with her when she had a baby, or see her become a doctor, and that their silly and endearing fun time and discussions were over. The fundamental need for a daughter to have her mother to turn to, would never happen again.

Jeanette and her husband got into the car and headed back up. As they were pulling onto her mom's street, they saw a funeral van in front of them, and Jeanette screamed, "No, oh No! Please pass them and tell them to give us some time before they come in to get her."

They found her mom sitting up on the bed, her mouth open, with a cloth wrapped around her head so her jaw would not sag. Jeanette knew immediately that her mom would not like that but also respected her Gram's history and former ways of doing things. Everyone was still sitting around the bed, most weeping quietly, all with very sad faces. Jeanette went to her bed to hug and kiss her mom and hold her one more time.

Three years later, Jeanette received a phone call from her very close Aunt and her Gram asking if she would fly up to be with them for Thanksgiving. They wanted to see her son who had been born the year before and was now sixteen months old.

Jeanette remembered the day Daniel was about eight months old and she was looking at him. He was dressed in a baby-blue shirt with a checkered blue-and-white romper with the biggest smile any baby could have. She felt another wave overtake her, but this one was different. It was a wave of pure love, so powerful it always remained part of her soul. She remembered thinking, *this is what real love is*. It totally enveloped her; she had never felt anything like it before. She so loved her son.

She was delighted to fly up to see her Gram and her aunt, accompanied by baby Daniel and her little sister, the one she felt so responsible for after she was born. Since she was thirteen years older than her, and their mom had passed away, Jeanette felt she had to step into her mom's place and be a protector for her sister. They arrived a few days before Thanksgiving, which had always been a special holiday in her family. Gram and Aunt both bustled around when they arrived, making sure everything was exactly right for them. Gram was now living in a downstairs bedroom, having abandoned her room upstairs for a time due to the stairs. But today she insisted on climbing those stairs to make sure everything was perfect.

Jeanette loved those days before Thanksgiving Day with her Gram. Having tea and toast every morning and usually afternoons too. Her Gram had emigrated to the United States from England when she was three years old, so all things English had passed down to Jeanette like a magical part of her DNA. Daniel got to feel the warm embrace of his Gram though he wouldn't remember it, but perhaps essences of love can be incorporated into one's being. Jeanette was very close to her grandmother. They had shared bedrooms and even a bed for most of her childhood. She wrote to her Gram frequently and loved picking out presents for her. Her Gram wrote her letters back, and they would talk on the phone regularly.

On Thanksgiving morning Jeanette and her Gram sat together and talked, with tea of course, for several hours. It was wonderful. That whole Thanksgiving Day was wonderful.

Until it wasn't.

At about 1:00 a.m. after all had gone to their respective beds, Jeanette was awakened by a rather frantic knock on the door. Daniel remained asleep by her bed. It was her aunt who told her that her Gram looked like she had had a heart attack, and the paramedics were called. By the time she got downstairs, they were at the door. They put her Gram on the floor so they could get to her easily, and asked Jeanette to stay with them so she could help. They wanted Jeanette to hold up an IV bag while they prepared to try to shock her heart with paddles. They did this several times with Jeanette watching every movement. Finally, they said they were going to transport her to the hospital—but it didn't look good.

A few hours later, Gram had passed away. Even though it came as no surprise to Jeanette, it was still devastating. In their talk on Thanksgiving morning, it was apparent how much her Gram wanted to see Jeanette and her wonderful baby before she left this Earth. Jeanette *knew* that after having this wish fulfilled, she was ready to let go, onto the place she believed was the next phase of her eternal life. She gave herself permission to move on.

The next day Jeanette sat in her Gram's upstairs bedroom and tried to inhale her grandmother. She looked through all the drawers of the beautiful red mahogany furniture, hoping to absorb her essence and know her even more deeply. She discovered a deep drawer that held all of Jeanette's many letters to her Gram. Another drawer held many of the presents Jeanette had sent to her over the years. Were they too precious to use? That alone time with Gram and her spirit helped Jeanette enormously. She knew that her Gram was a good person—a really good person. She was true to herself and her beliefs, always kind, and a fantastic depiction of a selfless person.

Another few years went by and Jeanette had an odd sensation in her left leg that she had never felt before. It was as if she was sustaining an electric shock on a two-inch square section of her leg just below the knee. She had no idea what was causing it and eventually was referred to a neurologist for examination and specific testing. The day of the examination she was given testing where the speed of electrical impulses was measured after needle shocks were given to various portions of her legs. The neurologist was sure she knew what it was and explained to her that she had a genetic disease that affected her peripheral nervous system. She told her the name of the disease for which there was no cure. After learning this, Jeanette returned to one of the schools she had worked at when out of the office.

The first thing she did was call her own office and ask Connie, one of the psychologists, to go into her office and find a book about rare diseases that she had on her bookshelf. Jeanette had always had rather unusual looking feet as a child; basically, her feet were deformed, but not that bad at that time. Connie found the disease in the book, and Jeanette asked her friend to read it to her over the phone.

Connie started but then hesitated saying, "Are you sure you want me to read this to you …why don't we wait until you get back to the office."

"Yes, please go ahead and read it to me," said Jeanette.

It was devastating. The disease caused progressive atrophy of the muscles in the legs and arms, and there was no formal treatment or anything that could be done for it. Many sufferers would end up in a wheelchair or would have much difficulty walking and require assistive devices to move around as they aged and the disease got worse. She was in her late thirties, and this was a big blow to her. It did explain why she felt less coordinated than others at times as a child and adolescent and hated gym in school. This was one more thing for Jeanette to research and learn about. Later, her father was determined to have the disease as well as her brother.

She was at the same school months later when she got a phone call informing her that something terrible had happened to her little sister, the one she had felt so responsible for when she was born and felt even more need to take care of after their mother's early death. Jeanette's sister had driven to a shopping area to get some aspirin for a headache, and when walking back to her car was kidnapped by five men, pushed to the floor of the back seat, and driven two counties away. There were witnesses that saw it happen, so police were alerted quickly.

This was a big story on the news in the Atlanta area. There were helicopters looking for her. Jeanette felt surreal realizing that this was her little sister and imagining her fear and the horror of what she was experiencing. Jeanette's sister, Lacy, was a tiny thing, very petite, and at most one hundred five pounds. The five men took her to a secluded area where she was gang raped by all five of them. Jeanette was also very worried about her stepdad who had lost his wife and now was dealing with such an atrocious act on his daughter.

The five men drove her back to the county where she was abducted and tossed her out of the car by the side of a road leaving her on the ground, where she was later found and taken to the hospital. When Jeanette finally got to be with her alone, she was amazed at the strength and relative composure she showed. What a horrid experience! The men were found and arrested and then Lacy had to go through the trial. These men were what some would call hillbilly dirt. They began a campaign with their own family members to threaten her and the family to try to influence the outcome of the trial. It didn't work. All the men were convicted and sent to jail with long sentences. But Jeanette's little sister paid a heavy price; she couldn't trust men anymore, and this would stay with her most of her life. Jeanette found herself in a mom-protective role, taking chances others wouldn't take for many years after this incident as her sister faced more obstacles to her emotional health. But like Jeanette, her little sister is a strong woman.

Jeanette found her second real love with the birth of her beautiful and adorable little daughter. She was like heaven in a pure bundle of sweetness. Jeanette's first real love, her son Daniel, just adored his new little sister. As they grew up together, they were each other's best friends, and Daniel became her protector. There were some very important things to protect her from. Jeanette and her daughter had the closest love imaginable. They simply adored one another, loved to play and do things together, spent tons of cuddle time, and were so proud of each other and let it be known. Except with Daniel, Jeanette had never known such love and the depth of love that was with her whenever she was with her daughter. Lots of silliness and special time together. Everyone loved her. She was a super star student, literally, winning that coveted honor at the end of the seventh grade. Most importantly, she was known to her classmates as the one person who would always help them, who was incredibly kind, and would not allow gossip or mean words to be said about anyone else in her presence. She was beautiful, but her inner beauty and goodness far surpassed her angelic outer beauty. If a mother and daughter could be *in love*, these two were over the moon.

By this time Jeanette and her husband were divorced and shared custody of the children. Jeanette bought a new house, and Daniel later said that that is the house he thinks of when he remembers home. She honored the commitment she had insisted on that each parent would refrain from saying anything negative about the other parent, but she later learned that wasn't the case in the other home. During Daniel's senior year, he had won incredible national awards in science and had to travel all over the country because of that. Around Christmas time, due to a snafu at her physician's office, Jeanette had a scare about the possibility of breast cancer, the cancer that had killed her mother. After that she began to have feelings/premonitions about something very bad happening in her family. Her daughter began having these too and wanted her mom to sleep with her near the end of the summer. There were also numerous occurrences whose meanings could only be discerned when one looked back and immediately saw their significance.

After her scare with breast cancer was corrected, she began to have concerns about Daniel and something happening to him on those many trips he had to take. However, by the summer, nothing had happened, so she was very relieved. Her time with her daughter that summer was magnificent. Her daughter had just been elected to be the President of the Beta Club at her school and had just decided to try out for her first ever musical theater production in community theater. Mom and daughter spent beautiful hours together lying on her bed, singing together, and rehearsing the songs so she could prepare for the tryouts. Mom attended all the tryouts with her, and she kept getting called back. They were both so excited. At the final tryout, Jeanette sat in the audience in the big performance theater and got to see her daughter in action. Wow! She was overwhelmed at her poise and her talent. Later that day they received a call saying that she had been given a great role and was also chosen as the backup for the main role of *Mary in the Secret Garden*. They jumped up and down; she was marvelous in the productions. On opening night, she was amazed when little girls came up to her afterward and asked for her autograph. Of course, Mom had a big bouquet of flowers for her star. In this production, Jeanette's daughter played the role of a spirit, helping Mary communicate with her deceased mother.

It was fairly late in the evening, about five o'clock on a Friday, and Jeanette had just finished a therapy session with a male Delta Airlines pilot. She received a phone call that changed her life forever. It was a woman who said Jeanette's son had asked her to call her. There had been an accident. Jeanette had been expecting the kids at any second since Daniel would be driving them both home after school. Jeanette called her ex-husband, told him, and said to get to the site immediately. She then called her present husband at work and told him to meet her at the hospital. Jeanette was frantic but still in control of her senses. The site of the accident was just blocks away. Traffic was backed up all four ways to the intersection where it had happened, so Jeanette had no choice but to drive on the wrong side of the road to get there.

What if somebody slams into me since I am driving on the wrong side of the road? I don't care. I need to get to my children.

As she approached the intersection, she suddenly felt as if she was in a movie. She seemed to be watching what was happening from a distance away. She imagined the people in all the cars saying, "That must be the mother."

It didn't appear real; it was a movie. As her car approached the intersection, a policeman quickly ran over to intercept her. He had another policeman take her keys to drive her car into the parking lot of a nearby service station. It was so quiet, so eerily quiet. The police officer asked her to get in his car so he could take her to the hospital. They began a trip that would remain forever vivid in her mind. Jeanette knew that her son was still alive since he had given her phone number to the woman who called her.

During the fifteen—minute ride to the hospital, she asked the officer several times if he knew anything about her daughter. He responded, "No," and "We will be there soon."

Then she felt it. She knew that her wonderful daughter

was gone. She asked the officer again, and this time he said, "It was bad."

They arrived at the hospital, and Jeanette was put into a small room cut off from everybody else. She supposed that this was to provide her privacy, but she felt so alone.

Her husband arrived, and that was some comfort. She heard a ruckus outside the room and later found out that her first husband had started a confrontation with the driver of the van who had hit them. He had just arrived by ambulance. Apparently, he complained of injuries during the wreck and insisted upon being admitted to the hospital.

The worst part was waiting an hour and a half just to be told how her children were. Jeanette asked several times for someone to come and talk to her, but no one did. She thought she was going to lose her mind. She couldn't sit still; she was pacing. Finally, a doctor appeared and stoically said, "Your son is being treated for injuries." Then in a cold, dispassionate manner said, "Your daughter is deceased."

Jeanette could not believe the way she had been told this awful truth by this—in her mind—"so-called doctor." Not one ounce of compassion; not even a touch on her hand. Nothing. Maybe she just needed to be mad at somebody, but she couldn't take this man.

He then had the audacity to say to her, "Do you want me to tell your son that his sister has died?" Jeanette looked him directly in the eyes and shouted, "Don't you dare! Now you take me right now to see my daughter. Right now."

The doctor got a nurse to take her to where her daughter was lying on a bed as if asleep. Still very beautiful with a clean white blanket gently pulled over her as if she was tucked in for bed at home. There was no indication that she was hurt at all. Jeanette stayed right at her head, leaned down, and told her how much she loved her. She caressed her face and kissed her, then began caressing her cheeks. As she did this a warm, red tiny stream of blood ran from her mouth onto Jeanette's hand. The warmth was like a message of the warmth of her daughter, her essence of kindness, of goodness, of love for all people. Suddenly, Jeanette felt as if a covering or a blanket was coming down on her from above, covering her with love and warmth, and she heard in her mind, "It's alright. It is alright."

She felt such a sense of peace then; it's very hard to put into words. But she knew it was real and comforting as the most joyful hug or envelopment that one could ever experience. She doesn't know if it was her daughter speaking to her or God or both. But it had a profound effect on her for the rest of her life.

Jeanette then went to find her son who was sitting in a hallway, alone in a room at the back of the emergency section, in a wheelchair. He looked younger than his eighteen years, banged up pretty bad but conscious. Jeanette knelt down to be at eye level with him, and when he saw her, his first words were, "How is she?"

Jeanette took his hand and with the other hand caressed his cheek and said, "She didn't make it, sweetheart."

The look on his face as the tears started to roll down his face would break any mother's heart.

They were told Daniel still needed more treatment but would be able to go home. Jeanette's daughter had to be sent to another county to have an autopsy. That didn't bother Jeanette as much as it may bother others. Ironically, Jeanette and her daughter had often watched the TV show *Autopsy* together as they were both so science-oriented and Jeanette's daughter seemed destined to be a doctor or something similar. Jeanette also read the full autopsy report, and it confirmed the injury she had anticipated, and the fact that she had died instantly. The police officer knew she was dead on the ride up to the hospital, but Jeanette greatly respected him for keeping it to himself.

Other police maybe not so much. Since they didn't know for sure "in their minds" what had caused the accident, they decided to take Daniel to the jail for processing as soon as he could leave the hospital.

This was unbelievable!

This happened even though the person who caused the accident was admitted by his own insistence so couldn't be taken to jail yet. The man was speeding and had run a red light to plow into their car slamming into the passenger side door. There was even a sheriff stopped at the red light who saw the van in the lane beside him run the light and speeding, and they had his statement as well as several others.

Life is sometimes unbearably unfair. So, Jeanette found

herself getting attorneys just after the accident to protect her son who had done nothing wrong and hiring an accident reconstructionist from Georgia Tech to prove that the accident was totally the other driver's fault.

Jeanette worried so much about her son. Here he was an eighteen-year-old honor student, who was acclaimed by his state and nation for such excellence in science, and just beginning his freshman year at the University of Georgia. He had just lost his best friend, his sister, and no matter how much Jeanette tried to tell him he did nothing wrong, she knew he would have survivors' guilt that could haunt him his whole life. She wanted him to take off a semester, at least, and stay with her. But Daniel was determined and wanted to stay in school.

Jeanette made a commitment to herself and to her daughter that she would live her life as her daughter was already living hers and continue with a now even more important purpose in life to help others. She also knew that she had to discover a way to live now that would help her manage to get through this unbearable grief.

She read over two-hundred books on death, conceptions of the afterlife, continued her voracious study of near-death experiences, read religious viewpoints, survival of consciousness research and studies of after death communication. Jeanette had to develop her own understanding of what she believed; no one could tell her what to believe. She had to experience it.

Jeanette also had extraordinary experiences of communication with her daughter that reaffirmed what she was already learning to believe. There comes a stage where the evidence is so very strong that belief turns into *knowing*. Once this knowing occurs, one becomes solid in their own belief system. And that feeling is marvelous. Jeanette is a very spiritual person, not necessarily a religious person, but spirituality so amazingly strong. She is also highly intuitive and focused on feelings. It is easy for her to *feel* the feelings of others around her. That can be a strength but also a heavy burden.

Jeanette also made the conscious decision that her daughter would remain in her life each and every day. She would talk to her and placed pictures all around the house to facilitate this. She also wrote articles and gave speeches to help others understand what it is like to lose a child, and also wanted friends, other psychologists, family, and religious and counseling professionals to know what really helps and what doesn't. There is absolutely no question that the death of a child is the most painful and horrific thing that can happen to a person. It is as if your entire world has collapsed and you cannot understand how ordinary things go on. You feel so lost—and you are lost because the part of you that lived in your child is gone. So, you feel that a part of your very self has died. Where is that love? You can't grasp it, you can't see it, you can't hear it, you can't taste it. However, you can FEEL it if you allow yourself to do so.

People have all kinds of ways to live with grief. However,

it is always a choice. Jeanette knew, that for her, it was to keep her daughter close to her—always. Some may try to put it totally out of their minds because it is too painful. That generally doesn't work in the end. Some cannot find a way out of despair and may even decide to take their own life. Jeanette already knew that her purpose in life was to help others. It was clear as a bell. So, she decided to focus on the positive; the wonderful person her daughter was and how in the short thirteen years she was here, she exuded such admirable values, kindness and care for others, appreciation for learning, and strength it often takes many a lifetime to learn, if they learn that at all. She would write, honor her daughter in this way, open eyes to the realization that love never dies and love is the most important gift in this world. Where there is love, there is goodness. Where there is love, there is hope, and where there is love, there is the promise of infinite joy.

Sages

"**O**H MY! OH MY!" Ellie covered her face with her hands. "Jeanette has had so much tragedy and heartache in her life. That is an incredible amount both of sorrow and grief as well as responsibility to be faced with. How in the world has she done that and still be standing?"

"Not only is she still standing but in many ways thriving. I'm amazed. Let's see if we can figure out how she did this," said Franklin. "The first thing she had going for her was her work. As professional as it was as a neuropsychologist, she absolutely loved her work. For over forty-five years she devoted herself to high standards and principles and received most of her gratification from what now seems apparent—from helping people. Robbie was the same way."

Ellie agreed. "Jeanette also made commitments to herself. She vowed to live her life as her daughter would, so admiring her caring for others, her natural kindness, her love of learning, and her intolerance for putting other people down.

When one can make commitments to oneself and keep them, that is a sign of strength. Jeanette is also the kind of person who needs to find meaning in everything. That's part of her personality. She studies, learns, analyzes, and then concludes about what something means. You must be very introspective to do that."

"You know what just hit me, Ellie? Both Jeanette and Robbie were like detectives. If you took their careers, they were actually doing the same thing—just in different venues. Both knew that you had to carefully assess and find where a student or client was on various attributes and then make decisions about what would work for them. Then, they each had to design the right approaches to help this person. Both of them also needed to have *proof* that what they were recommending would actually work and be helpful. They both relied heavily on independent research, constant learning, and an open mind."

"There's something else that is really coming clear, Franklin. Both Robbie and Jeanette put other people's feelings and needs above their own. Look at Robbie's work in North Vietnam and later in Thailand—all that wonderful work. Do you know how their organization funded that work? Robbie and his cohorts would sell refreshments at all the Georgia Tech football games or other stadium events."

Franklin said, "I didn't know that. But it doesn't surprise me about Robbie. I know something about Jeanette that most people don't know either. Two days after her daughter was killed in the accident where the other driver was speeding and ran a red light, she called the business he was working for and asked to speak to him. She explained to his boss that she was very concerned about his welfare, especially since there was so much in newspapers and TV about the accident and her daughter. She told him that she wanted to forgive him because she thought that would help him. But his boss said that they had been advised by their attorneys not to speak to her."

An opportunity to help denied.

"You know there is a word that could be used to describe these two. It's *selfless*. They don't know that it is an apt word right now, but it is going to become paramount for both of them in the future. I'm kind of glad that we know more of what's to come than they do right now."

"A lot of the similarities we previously talked about regarding these two are really standing out now. Things like both feeling high levels of responsibility and both showing good leadership."

"Also, their high standards and principles and determination to stick to them. Remember, they both quit their jobs and moved on to something better when their autonomy was threatened as well as what they believed it. Both were quite brave in their own ways. Yes, they both felt that sticking to their own values and beliefs was more important than keeping a job. They think very much the same."

"Yes…you would think they were soulmates, Ellie."

"Very funny, Franklin."

Robbie

WHEN ROBBIE WAS WORKING with his clients in the gyms for his second career, he always felt more at home than in his own home. This was one of the reasons he insisted on calling his clients *friends*. He was rather adamant about it. Everyone in the gym could see that he was not like the other *trainers* or *coaches,* and folks would often make remarks about it or approach him asking what he was doing. He was a scientist who devoted himself to helping others get better in whatever would contribute to their having a fulfilling and healthier life. He was a data nerd, as any good scientist is, constantly measuring, recording, and interpreting just how well his friend/client was progressing toward their mutual goals. It would be quite rare to see a trainer with a clipboard and a carefully designed program individualized to that one person in a gym with the trainer actually recording data. He was definitely different.

It didn't take long, after embarking on this new career,

for lots and lots of people to notice the way he worked, the care he gave to each individual, and the actual friendship that really did happen with the folks he worked with. Besides, he was quite likable and made others feel that he truly cared about them. Robbie's work with his clients did not end in the gym. At night and sometimes on weekends, he would analyze all his recorded data to determine whether specific changes needed to be made or if he should add other exercises to advance or address a new issue. That was just as important as the initial plan for each individual.

Before long Robbie found himself working with an enormous number of people along with working on himself. If anyone asked him why he had so many clients, he would probably say, "How can I turn anyone away?"

He would sometimes take on clients for no charge using the very same sentence. Research was also a very important part of his working with others. Robbie was never satisfied with what he already knew. He had to learn more, to look at every angle that could help a person, to get better at what he could do. Robbie never stopped learning; he was the very definition of a *lifetime learner.*

Just like when he was the high school principal at *gang central*, Robbie's approach was very different from the common, traditional practice. He was way ahead of everyone else. Over time he began working with an older population with a far different and complex arena of needs and priorities. He found himself working with people in wheelchairs, with muscular disorders, with neurological problems like stroke or other brain injuries. Unfortunately, many of these people had been through traditional physical therapy after an injury or event but didn't really progress, rather remained incapacitated. Some had been given up on. Perhaps placed on so many different medications that their *illness* had the cause of medication-induced dementia or medication-induced motor problems. These situations were very demoralizing for Robbie as he wanted to help everyone, and if there was a chance that he could do that—he wanted to not just give it a try but the most informed and best try he could give.

That was the nature of Robbie and why he was so appreciated. However, there was a dark cloud hanging over him. A dark cloud that had so influenced his sense of self and had him questioning himself once he left his home at the gym and his clients/friends.

What was this dark cloud made of? Why did it keep him from realizing what a really good man he was? Why couldn't he see through the inky waves obstructing his vision?

Here was a man who in one venue looked to be an extraverted, extremely caring individual who always loved to make people smile and almost always had a quick smile on his face. A man who always seemed to be in his element in this venue, who deliberately made friends out of acquaintances, who appeared relaxed and interested in the lives and needs of others. He was fun to be around and could easily talk to anyone.

However, put him in a different environment and he

seemed a different man. For example, Robbie hated parties; he avoided them if at all possible. He couldn't stand large groups and meaningless chit-chat or cocktail party conversation. Robbie didn't like silly games a group would play or doing something that didn't have any purpose. He was very much into nutrition and so hardly ever went out to eat and certainly didn't enjoy it when he did.

But the most meaningful characteristic of this man Robbie, was his very strong inclination to be self-critical. Perhaps this started with his critical and disparaging father who never said a good word about him, or to him. As he went through life, and especially in his second career, it was so easy for him to demean himself to himself, for anything that anyone could take as a negative act. He was also super sensitive to actions, words, sounds, or inactions suggesting he did something wrong and he was being disparaged.

However, Robbie didn't want to let those feelings out. He may have been afraid of his own anger or thought less of himself for having such feelings. When one keeps such feelings inside, they tend to build resentment. And then what do you do with that?

Robbie simply didn't know himself. He had no idea what a good man he was. He didn't know how to express true feelings as he had buried his own for most of his life. Robbie had no idea what love was. He did know the love of his mother which likely saved him. But true love between a man and a woman was foreign to him. He couldn't even imagine what it would feel like. He didn't know—but he *so* wanted to know.

Robbie didn't get married until he was in his thirties. He was introduced to his wife by a mutual friend, and they dated for a while before deciding to get married. She was pretty, and there were qualities in her that he admired. She had been married before and had a young daughter who would later get married and have four children. They also had one daughter together. Robbie's first recollection of love occurred when he was holding his daughter for the first time. It was like a wave of pure love rolled over him; a feeling he had never felt before. It was exquisite and powerful. He felt such responsibility for his daughter's welfare; it was his duty to protect her.

Robbie thought he was in love when he first married. A lot of people go through this in both wishful thinking and pretend love, probably a majority of people. It can lead to a very positive outcome, overtime, of really being in love but also may be a symptom of false expectations and less insight into what love really should be. Often one or both parties in a marriage really try to make it work in the beginning, but the differences between them are like a deep crevice in a mountain that expands over time.

Robbie's sense of duty followed him throughout his married life. When his wife's daughter from her previous marriage found herself in a terrible situation with what appeared to be a narcissistic father to the four children, she got a divorce and moved into Robbie and his wife's house. Characteristically, Robbie criticized himself for not seeing the true character of this man. All of this family of five came under the support of Robbie. He had huge financial and personal responsibility for this large group of people.

Although Robbie certainly appreciated many of his wife's qualities, there were some that caused him much distress. He saw her as being a very good teacher as she homeschooled all those grandchildren. He saw her as a good person in several ways, but over time began to resent that he was always taken for granted, never felt appreciated for all that he did, and never felt loved.

His usefulness seemed to stem only for what he could do for her as she was always telling him to do things around the house or for the household. He also felt the duty to protect her as she had a physical disability that put her at great risk for falling and potentially hurting herself seriously. Again, he saw that as his duty. However, they had very little in common, had no real shared interests, and personalities that didn't seem to mesh together at all. He didn't blame her for this, rather just accepted it as a fact.

For twenty-two years they had not shared the same bed-room and had no intimacy at all. Robbie *lived* in a small bedroom that also doubled as his office. He would retreat there most of the time, did not share meals with the rest of those living there as he didn't eat the same kinds of foods. He prepared all his own meals. Robbie was very serious about nutrition and continuous research to assure that he was con-suming the very best for his body. The others in the family group were not interested. Over time, he felt like a workhorse whose only value was doing what he was told to do and making the money to support all of these people, with no or very little appreciation for his contributions.

In addition, Robbie was the kind of person who planned effectively and needed to have things organized. That was a cornerstone of his personality. He could not stand chaos and disorganization around him. So, he found himself constantly washing dishes that had been left in the sink or around the house by the others, and because no one else cared to clean, he took on that job as well. He washed his own clothes, did the yardwork, took care of the cars, and ran errands. For a long time, he never really self-reflected or examined his own feelings and thoughts but was aware of the deepening resentment he was feeling. It got to the point where the dichotomy between his second career life in the gym and his life at home was so stark that he didn't even want to go home.

Robbie was afraid of his own feelings. He kept them hidden—behind a mask; he in no way wanted to be like his father and would be self-critical if his internal feelings did not match the way he wanted to be. He had very little understanding of who he really was. He would chastise himself if he didn't meet some internal expectations of who he should be, thus putting enormous pressure on himself. He didn't see himself as a good man, although, that was what he yearned to be. As negative thoughts began to dominate, he didn't appreciate himself. He also yearned for love, although, it would be difficult for him to put that need and desire into words for some time. He really did not know what love was. He was so used to receiving negative messages constantly from his wife, that at first it contributed to his self-criticism and later to a fast-growing body of resentment that was beginning to take over his life.

The one thing that was solid with Robbie was his spiritual relationship with God. It was important to differentiate between religious and spiritual. Robbie would say that he is not actually religious, although he enjoys going to church and getting meaning from what he hears. He would define religion as living through a set of rules. Having a close personal relationship with God was a spiritual matter and was different. He so wanted to be the kind of man who would please God. But his self-criticism kept him from recognizing the good man he actually was. He did recognize that he did good things but thought that all the negative thoughts he had during his life would not be acceptable to God. Robbie did feel that he knew his purpose in life—to help others. That was clear. And how did he help others? Through his work, making people laugh at the grocery store, by bringing a little joy to a stranger's life with kindness, going out of his way to comfort someone at the gym, and many, many other small acts of caring.

It was time for Robbie to learn what a good man he really was.

Jeanette

Back when Jeanette was in undergraduate and then in graduate school, there was a lot of pressure to get married. The last thing any woman seemed to want was to leave the university without a marriage partner picked out. Jeanette felt that pressure too but also wanted a career. She had met her first husband through her little sister in her sorority who was at that time a sweetheart sister for one of the fraternities at Georgia Tech. Jeanette and her sorority little sister had an apartment and invited several people over for a casual dinner including both sorority and fraternity members. She thought she was going to be paired up with a fellow she liked but ended up with one of his fraternity brothers. They talked easily, and by the time the party was ending, he asked if she would like to go down to Georgia Tech and talk some more. They ended up at the Georgia Tech stadium, stayed up all night talking, and then watched the sun come up.

Summer was coming up, and these two started dating. They saw each other frequently, and Jeanette was fascinated by him. Antonio came from another country, seemed very intelligent, was interested in music, taping, and could maintain a good conversation.

However, there were plenty of red flags waving about this relationship. First there were cultural differences; he had an entire family living in Florida that had emigrated from Cuba when Castro took over. They had been very rich in Cuba but now had little money since they had to leave so suddenly. Her mom and Gram told her that she didn't have to get married, but her soon-to-be husband announced that he was about to be drafted and then sent to Vietnam. Back then that was an extremely scary proposition.

Another red flag occurred when his cousin who was attending Harvard, came down for a visit and decided to stay for a couple of months. He was an intriguing character, and people were impressed that he attended Harvard. He asked Jeanette to set him up for a date with one of her sorority sisters. Jeanette didn't see anything wrong with this and so arranged for him to go out with the sweetest of all her sorority sisters, and they began dating regularly.

What Jeanette didn't know was this Harvard guy was already married to an American woman living in Boston. Jeanette was mortified when she found out and sickened that her soon-to-be husband Antonio knew this all along and had gone along with his cousin. She had to tell her sorority sister the truth and apologized profusely for what had happened. Certainly not a strong beginning.

Jeanette's boyfriend Antonio was drafted into the Army and would soon leave for boot camp. She had a health scare, and her boyfriend took this occasion to bring her a beautiful engagement ring, though she can't recall that he actually asked her to marry him. She was impressed as well as a little groggy and accepted the ring. Jeanette thought she was in love, though she really didn't know what love was. Often, in those days and probably continuing through to the present time, very few young people had any understanding of what true love is. Most love fell into one of two categories: 1) Wishful thinking or 2) Pretend love.

Jeanette was a rescuer. She had such empathy for people and always wanted to rescue or heal them. It started back at eight years old when she had her pet clinic. She knew that her fiancé was going to go to Vietnam after boot camp and AIT and that he was scared. He wanted to have someone to love when he went. She remembered what had happened to her former boyfriend who was killed after she told him she wasn't ready to get married and didn't rescue him.

So, her mom put together a sweet wedding for them in October of 1969; he was given leave to come home and get married.

Jeanette soon found herself living in a trailer on a farm in Missouri with the wife of another soldier. They lived in this isolated place and only saw their husbands on rare occasions.

Her husband learned that he could apply for Officer Candidate School housed in Fort Benning in Columbus, Georgia. This could delay his going to Vietnam for eighteen weeks, so he took it. They bought a little yellow Volkswagen Bug and headed off.

Jeanette needed to find housing off base for herself. She had one day only to do this with her husband by her side. She also had to learn how to drive the little bug, get a job, arrange for all the utilities for the apartment she had found, get her driver's license, and find her way around Columbus, Georgia, so she could drive to work and find her way around the base. She had to do all of it in one day. Jeanette would not be allowed to see her husband for ten weeks except on Sunday for church. Public displays of affection or PDA's were not allowed there.

It was a very busy day. When she went to the employment office in downtown Columbus, they first told her that they had nothing that matched her qualifications. But, someone standing nearby interjected that the Office of Planning and Development just upstairs was looking for someone. So up the stairs she went. The director asked her if she took dictation and if she was a good and fast typist. She said she had skills in that area. He then asked her to come into his office and take a letter. As he dictated, she wrote things on the steno pad out of his sight. It was not shorthand but, in her mind, close enough. She also had a good memory. He then asked her to type it in the office outside of his.

Jeanette had learned a system where she would type extra letters or spaces so it would sound like she was a fast typist. Back then they did not have the silent keyboards and computers of today. She never had learned to type like other people; she just was pretty fast but still had to look at the keyboard. The director was pleased and hired her on the spot.

She was now the administrative assistant to the Head of the Criminal Justice Division. Her first job was to write a grant for a new helicopter for the Columbus Police Department. She completed everything she was supposed to do that day.

Her husband was ready to graduate from OCS, and all the wives went to the parking lot for a fifteen-minute time with their husbands, and all were told they didn't need as many officers as predicted. So, they offered them all guaranteed stateside duty, and cut off one year on their enlistment, if they took the offer to resign from OCS. They were expecting about 15 percent to take it. Surprise! 95 percent took it. There was jubilation in that parking lot.

Now Jeanette and her husband were off for a year to Manhattan, Kansas, which is close to a major base. There was a state university there, and it was a pretty college town in a landscape of brown grass and drabness. Jeanette had asked her Dean of Admissions at her university to get in touch with his equal at the Kansas university for an introduction, and they proceeded to his house when they arrived. There wasn't anything available in the Admissions Department, but the couple were just getting ready to take a long trip overseas and asked if they would like to house sit while they were gone.

Jeanette found a job as an office manager for an orthopedic surgeon. It was a good job, and she did quite well at it. Shortly after the homeowners returned, Antonio was sent to Germany for two months of maneuvers. She was beginning to realize that she really didn't know her husband at all. They hardly spent any time together. While he was gone, she found another apartment that suited them better and started painting orange crates from the grocery store yellow to use as bedside tables. When he came home, he felt like a stranger. They spent a year there.

When he was finally discharged, they headed back to Atlanta. Jeanette had two courses to finish before getting her undergraduate degree, and her husband had a few more, mostly in English. Jeanette found a full-time job at a company that sold, of all things, service station equipment. She started as a secretary/receptionist but kept moving up until she was given the job of actually working with those needing their equipment as a sales representative. They never had a female sales representative before. It was fun being with all the guys, but it didn't require much creativity.

One day, on her own, she started designing collection notices like no one had ever seen before. She made humorous cards with funny artwork to gently remind customers of their debt, and the president and vice president of the company liked them so much they made her their new Advertising

Manager. They moved her to an office in the shipping department and got her a printer—a huge thing. Remember computers were just in somebody's head at this time, and printers were fossils with not much flexibility, but she loved it! The whole time she worked at this company she was attending graduate school at her university as well. She left after she got her master's degree and began working in the school system, but she took many fond memories with her.

Jeanette's husband wanted to go to graduate school at Georgia Tech to get a PhD in chemistry. So, she worked to support that dream for him. Occasionally, he would get a TA or Teaching Assistant small payment, but basically, she supported them both. The problem was her husband couldn't or wouldn't do anything. He spent five years working on his PhD and ended up with what he already had, an undergraduate degree in chemistry. Jeanette couldn't believe it but still tried to be supportive. She got him a job in her school system teaching high school chemistry.

Jeanette thought things might change when at age twenty-nine, she became pregnant. Her mom had passed away, so she was pretty much on her own. Her husband, who was fascinated with taking photos and movies, upgraded all his equipment in preparation for the big day. He was a very meticulous man. He would spend hours upon hours each night with elaborate systems for paying bills or cataloging things that didn't need such attention. She hardly saw him. He had left the school system since he thought the students were beneath his abilities. He did get another job as a paint chemist for a major paint company not far away from where they lived.

In the hospital room the delivery was proceeding slowly and painfully. Both her husband and her doctor spent all their time looking at his recording equipment, paying very little attention to the woman having the baby.

Jeanette knew there was something not quite right with her. Finally, when she could get the doctor's attention, he sent her for an X-ray. She was put in a wheelchair, and a nurse took her to x-ray and left her alone in the hall. Her husband did not go with her. She was in such pain, agony, wanting so much to scream. Suddenly, right after the X-ray, she was told she had to have an emergency C-section. And she wanted it—the pain was too hard to bear.

Soon, Jeanette's son, Daniel, was born, and this marked the beginning of her understanding what love is. Before long she was back in her room where her son would soon join her. She didn't know where her husband was. Finally, she was told that he had left the hospital because she had delivered a boy—and he wanted a girl.

He had stormed out as soon as he knew. She knew he was an intelligent man; that it is the father's sperm that determines the sex of the child—yet he blamed her for disappointing him. It was a huge revelation of the character of this man.

Daniel was such a wonderful baby, and Jeanette felt overwhelming love for him. He was the center of her life. Her husband began to gradually withdraw away from her. He gave her an indication he was interested in someone else.

There were stark differences between them. Throughout their marriage he never finished any of the projects they were trying to save money on when building the house. He spent more and more time alone in his makeshift office in the basement doing meticulous accounting. Intimacy was almost gone, and when it did happen, it was rough and demanding, not gentle and loving.

Finally, one day when Daniel was ten, he said to his mom, "Mommy, I never see you and Daddy showing any affection anymore."

That was it for Jeanette.

What am I teaching my children about love and marriage with this as a model.

She asked him for a divorce, and they began a very detailed document to split everything up and shared custody of Daniel and her daughter. The typed document was about three inches thick. They did not use an attorney but did have to go before a judge. He took one look at the document. "I don't have time to read all of this."

Then he looked at each of them. "Do you agree with everything in this document?"

He granted the divorce based on their affirmative answers.

Jeanette decided to leave the current house with him and bought a new one for herself. She later found out from her children, who were very distressed, that he constantly berated

Jeanette in front of them. He had agreed never to do this. He never kept up the house they had built in a nice neighborhood, rather, many years later, he just left it to rot.

Jeanette realized over the years that this marriage had been doomed from the beginning. She didn't really even know this man since their first years they barely saw one another when he was in the Army. She had been a rescuer to a man who as a child remembered a life of entitlement and overindulgence. He always had a fascination with young females so that others, including her mom and later her son, were hesitant about him being alone with them.

He was self-centered and could become enraged if something didn't go his way. Clearly, his values and beliefs were not like Jeanette's. That is essential for real love. As well as trust—which was also lacking.

Jeanette enjoyed being independent, loved her new house and the beautiful memories she made there with her children. It was good. Jeanette had arranged in the divorce to have considerably more quality time with her children than her ex-husband. After several years passed, she began to think about perhaps meeting someone. But how to do it? Back then there was no internet, no dating sites, so she somewhat hesitantly decided to put a little ad in the *Atlanta Journal*. This was the most common way people would meet, and it was pretty safe. People answering the ad would write her a letter, and the newspaper would forward all the letters received to her address. Jeanette thought she would maybe get a few at least, so why not?

She felt safe because she was in control. No one knew her name and address, and she would be the initiator by calling and then talking to a person she might be interested in meeting.

The first day she got letters there were about twenty of them—pretty good. She had a good time reading them. Within a week, she had hundreds and hundreds!

They ranged from doctors and dentists and big wigs in state government to artists, graphic designers, and even—believe it or not—several prisoners who accompanied their letter with full-frontal naked pictures. She had so much fun. Each day she would take her new letters to work, and during lunch, they would all read them and give a heads-up or not to a follow-up. It was like all her friends were involved. It was fun going out on a bunch of dates with a few becoming repetitive. The dentist lasted only two dates because he had lied when he said he didn't smoke—no trust there. She learned a lot about men and what she didn't want to get involved in through this experience. One of the artists hit her up for money within about an hour. Gone! Some tugged at her heart—one pretty big time. Then she read a letter that tugged at her heart in a different way—he would become her husband for three decades.

It was a sweet letter, and she could tell he had struggled to write what he wanted to say. She decided to call him and meet at a nearby restaurant. There were hardly any parking places left, and there were two cars positioned to get it—hers and the man she was meeting. He let her take the space. They had a beautiful dinner, and he asked if he could see her again. He lived quite a distance away but was willing to come to spend time with her.

So, they began dating regularly. He treated her well, liked showing her off to his friends where he lived, and had a nice apartment and a wonderful, beautiful daughter that he clearly adored. He knew what Jeanette was doing with all the letters she had received and referred to himself as being *on the bubble*, apparently a racecar reference.

Although she didn't know it at the time, this person was very competitive and after a short time realized that he would do anything to win the competition as he saw it. He was attentive, seemed to be a nice guy, got along pretty well with her kids, seemed so interested in her, and wanted to be with her. After a time, she gave him a bottle of bubble-making liquid and told him he was *off the bubble*.

After about a year, they decided to get married. Jeanette knew that he had money problems and needed *rescuing*—that should have been a big red flag. She did insist that he finish the bankruptcy he had started before the marriage so she wouldn't inherit any of his former debt. The wedding was beautiful and quite memorable. Both of their daughters were in the wedding party dressed in identical dresses, and her son had organized all the music for the wedding and the reception. It was held in a fabulous colonial house full of flowers and good friends. Everyone had a wonderful time.

The problems began on the day of the wedding, after the reception. They had planned a honeymoon in Maine and would spend the night in Atlanta before flying up there. Jeanette likened it to a switch that was turned off right after the wedding. Her husband showed no interest in her once they got to the hotel. All he wanted to do was watch TV, particularly golf; Jeanette couldn't believe it. It felt like he realized he had won the competition and now did not have to do anything anymore. He had been rescued and perhaps, in his mind, could be taken care of the rest of his life.

Much later Jeanette found a long letter she had written to him one year after the marriage. It is so much easier to see the light when looking backward over the many years they had been married. It was clear she was trying to make it work but let him know that she was distressed by his lack of attention to her and lack of any semblance of contribution to the marriage in terms of doing anything around the house, financially, or in an intimate relationship. He chose to retire at age fifty-five. Their marriage was not a marriage; Jeanette had supported him the entire time. Rather, they shared her house and thus were roommates.

Four years after the marriage Jeanette's beloved daughter was killed, and Jeanette suffered the greatest loss any parent could have. She devoted herself to her work and her promise to her daughter to live her life the way her daughter was doing. Jeanette received almost all her gratification from helping the many families and children she worked with. She had good friends through her work and professional organizations she was active in. She also devoted herself to helping people who had suffered great loss and assisting people who needed help but did not have the funds to pay for it.

She put up with living with a roommate instead of having a marriage.

As time went on, things got worse. Although she had been by his side during several major health concerns, her husband did not return the favor. He knew about her genetic progressive disease before they married, and as things became more difficult for her, he became more neglectful to the point that others noticed it. He would walk ten feet in front of her rather than trying to help with navigation. He seemed to resent that she had trouble walking without aid; she didn't know at first if this was because he was embarrassed by it or simply didn't want to put forth the effort to help her. Once he left her stranded in the rain and unable to get down a curb to get to the car because he had pulled so far away to pick her up. He made no effort to get out of the car to help her. Finally, an older couple approached her asking if she needed some help.

"I think I do."

They helped her down the curb for which she was thankful but also humiliated.

The most egregious event, however, occurred one day when she slipped on a wet area in her house onto a hard tile surface and seriously hurt herself. He was annoyed by her cries of pain and told her to just crawl to the bed and she would be alright.

He did not help her.

Jeanette knew she shouldn't move but he insisted. Finally, after trying, she asked him to call an ambulance, or give her her phone so she could call. When the paramedics got there, the first thing they said is that she never should have moved. The four paramedics carefully put her on a gurney and strapped her down. When they arrived at the hospital, they thought she was having a heart attack and treated that possibility first.

After several hours, they took x-rays and ordered an MRI first thing the next morning. They didn't see any broken bones but suspected significant internal damage. They couldn't do an MRI in the emergency room.

Early the next morning her husband pulled the car about ten feet out of the garage and opened the door to the passenger side, before he walked back into the garage. Jeanette used a walker to try to get into that side by herself, but both of her legs gave out, she fell backward and hit her head on the concrete driveway.

She laid crumpled on the driveway. Her husband, Rick, walked toward her, but when he was still at least six feet away, he said something that would remain embedded in her brain for the rest of her life.

He said, "I'm going back in the house. You crawl in when you're ready."

Jeanette could not believe it. Who would leave someone seriously hurt and unable to move, especially a husband—or even a roommate. He watched TV when he went back in the house.

Jeanette lay there thinking for about twenty minutes. She decided that she would get in the car one way or another. As soon as she could get to the MRI center, she would call her son Daniel who was living in another state and tell him what had happened. She knew he would get there as quickly as he could. She did not feel safe without her son.

Jeanette pondered that perhaps her husband wanted her to die. Or something was seriously wrong with him. After a while he appeared at the door to the garage.

She yelled at him, "Throw me that towel in the garage so I can try to get in the car."

He did but still stayed in the garage.

Jeanette maneuvered the towel and got on both knees to try to pull herself into the car. She knew she shouldn't do this but had no other choice. Through sheer willpower, she got herself in then yelled, "Now you take me to my MRI appointment."

When she arrived and was away from her husband, she called her son. He was on his way within thirty minutes.

The clinic informed her that both of her knees were dislocated. This likely happened when she got on her knees to get into the car. The MRI showed significant damage to her right leg as well as damage to her left leg. She was told to go home, stay in bed, and that she would need much rehabilitation.

When they got back home, Jeanette decided that she would say nothing to her husband until her son arrived. She didn't know how he would react, and she definitely did not feel safe.

Daniel got there in record time—five hours; Jeanette was so relieved. She and her son asked her husband why he had done such a thing. He had no explanation, and he didn't apologize. It was totally bizarre. Jeanette told him she did not want him in the house anymore, that he would have to leave. He resisted, but finally left, likely going to his daughter's.

Jeanette later called his daughter to ask her if he was there, and if she knew what had happened. It was obvious she was standing right next to him.

His daughter asked him, "Did you really do that?"

You could hear him through the phone, a somewhat shaky, "Yeh."

He stayed away for three days and then called and said he was coming home. She again told him she didn't want him there.

"It's my house too, and I am coming home."

She was so thankful her son was with her. He stayed for ten days.

After her son left, Jeanette tried to gently talk to her husband to try to figure out why he had done what he did.

He still could come up with no explanation.

Things continued to get worse. He became uncommunicative. He seldom initiated any conversation, would make disparaging gestures with his hand when she tried to talk to him, and continued to do nothing around the house to help her though she was still working full time and took care of everything. As a psychologist, Jeanette tried to determine what was going on with him, but that is very difficult to do when he wouldn't talk. He only wanted to do what he liked; play golf, watch TV in his own room, eat meals, especially going out for meals. That was about it. The two had frequently talked about divorce over the years.

He always responded, "You give me enough money, and I'm out of here."

Sages

"ROBBIE IS DEFINITELY AT A PRECIPICE emotionally, and it is time for something really big to happen and change his life. It's clear that Robbie doesn't know himself and has protected his feelings, even from himself. That's his mask. He is so self-critical, and you really can't blame him considering his background and life experiences."

"Absolutely, Franklin! And I really can see that he doesn't know what love is. Of course, Jeanette doesn't either. She has known for a while that she is a *rescuer* and the only real love she has known is the kind between her and her children. That is a treasured and extraordinarily special kind of love but not the same as between a man and a woman or other true unions. She fell victim to *wishful thinking love* and tried to make it work but after a while recognized the futility of it. Love cannot be one sided. That won't work."

"I think Robbie also had a *wishful thinking* kind of love. He really had no clue of what love feels like or even what it should feel like. Again, except for the love he felt for his daughter. He was so unhappy but found his meaning in the work he was doing. He had a gradual recognition that his purpose in life was to help other people," said Franklin. "Interestingly enough, Jeanette recognized that was also her purpose in life." He looked directly at Ellie. "They have the exact same purpose."

"Jeanette had an unbelievable amount of non-love and hurtful behavior from spouses for decades and decades. There's a pattern there—first rescue, then try very hard to make it work, find fulfillment in other areas like her work and her purpose, put up with disparaging, cruel behavior, for as long as she could. Then something would trigger the need to get away from the situation so she would finally act.

"Her life required much self-reflection, self-awareness, and deep thinking. Jeanette knew a lot about feelings, but that didn't stop her from making the wrong choices. Robbie went through life hiding his feelings from others and from himself. He needed help to open up to his feelings.

"Then Jeanette coped by building a huge set of armor around her to protect her from all of the external pain and threats to her inner self. It was solid and strong. Robbie hid behind his mask." Ellie thought for a second. "The true Robbie he so longed to be and the good man he already was, don't you think?"

"I do, and these life experiences had to happen for both of them, in order to learn the lessons that brought them to Earth for this human learning experience. They had to have exactly what happened to them to grow their souls. They both had to learn what love is and what it is not. Hard as they are, these life experiences were essential for them.

"Robbie needs to learn and *feel* what a truly good man he is, and Jeanette needs to *feel* what it's like to be cherished. To be loved for her real self, to be appreciated, and to be listened to."

Franklin sighed. "The idea of *motivation* behind actions is a very powerful tool in this learning for both of them. For example, if one were to examine the motivation behind the first of Jeanette's spouses, one is likely to find somebody to *pretend love.* He was going to Vietnam and needed to feel he had somebody at home because of his fear or loneliness. He also had a lot of personality concerns from his previous life of privilege, arrogance, and related serious difficulty of never finishing anything. His self-centeredness, anger when he didn't get his way. Then his need to control were major contributors to an unhappy marriage. He seemed to feel that everything should be given to him on a silver platter." He shook his head. "I'm glad Jeanette realized that was such a bad model for her children she so loved, and for her to divorce him.

"Then the second marriage followed the same pattern. It doesn't matter how smart a person may be, they can still fall victim to these mistakes. They may be empathetic and want to help other people, like Jeanette is. Some people see life only through the lens of what is good for them. Jeanette again rescued someone in trouble who was looking to be taken care of with no effort. Once he won the competition, he felt he didn't have to do anything at all.

"However, the result of this *pretend love* and this *motivation* is a growing level of resentment in both spouses. Jeanette's husband in the three-decade-long second marriage likely loved the situation at first, but over time began to resent it and her enormously. She was the successful one, the financial supporter, took care of everything, made most of the decisions because he was not interested or didn't want to put forth the effort. Jeanette also began to feel growing resentment but had to deal with incredible grief and literally had to find a way to live after the death of her daughter.

"Over time things just got worse and worse. He ignored her need for assistance because of her physical disability. He mocked her and refused to engage in any conversation because he didn't want to listen to what she had to say. He became increasingly petulant, childish, and finally, he engaged in cruelty.

"Almost all of Jeanette's second marriage involved living with a *roommate* who didn't pay rent, didn't do any work around the house, didn't contribute financially, but did say 'thank you' after she cooked dinner and served it to him. And never offered to clean up and showed no intimacy toward her for almost all of the marriage. There is considerable similarity between Robbie and Jeanette on this roommate dimension. In both situations, the spouses had little in common and did not share interests at all. Yes, it's apparent that both Robbie and Jeanette had not experienced real love between a man and a woman. Robbie could not even imagine what it felt like. Jeanette was a little better in this regard because she is an intuitive person and could at least imagine."

Franklin nodded. "Things are about to change quite dramatically. Will Jeanette and Robbie learn what love is? They have already learned what it is not."

Sages

POSTSCRIPT

JEANETTE WAS IN HER EARLY FORTIES when she finally found out the likely cause of her anxious behavior as a child. Remember how she hid from white cement trucks whenever they came on her street for years. She was afraid if they saw her—they would get her, and she would be gone. She also had continuous nightmares about the moon trying to get her and suck her up into oblivion if she was outside or even by a window in her house where the moon could see her.

One day Jeanette, wearing a read blazer, was attending a professional conference in North Atlanta. Although there were a lot of people there, the speaker seemed to zero in on her and referred to her as the lady in the red blazer. He asked her a question; although, she can't remember what it was. She found herself becoming increasingly anxious, anticipating the long drive home, and feeling uncomfortable in that environment.

On her way home while driving alone, she had a panic attack. It was extremely uncomfortable and scary, but she did finally make it home safely. That night she called her aunt and asked, "Did anything happen to me when I was a child that could cause me to have a panic attack and anxiety?"

Her aunt hesitated, was silent for too long, and then said, "I think you should ask your father."

Now she was really concerned. What in the world had happened to her? So, she called her dad up in Maryland and asked the same question.

He also hesitated. "Uh, I really don't want to tell you."

Her anxiety level was increasing with each second of silence. Finally, she said, "Dad, I really need to know this. It's important."

"Okay, when you were three years old, your mom and I were walking with you along a street where there was some traffic. Suddenly, a white cement truck came barreling down the road just as a little girl stepped into the street. The cement truck hit her and literally smashed her with it's incredible weight. It was such a horrific scene with red blood all over the road. We tried to shield your eyes, but you had seen the whole thing. We decided to never talk about it in any way. It probably wasn't the right decision."

"Thank you, Dad. I needed to know."

Remember, they had no idea what she was doing as a child hiding from cement trucks and having dreams about the white moon sucking her up into oblivion. They thought they were protecting her.

Now, for Jeanette as a neuropsychologist, she finally understood. She knew her sensitivity to the colors red and white in certain situations and now got it. She understood why she hid herself away from white cement trucks so they couldn't see her, even though she had no memory of it. Jeanette even understood the panic attack when she was driving after feeling uncomfortable at that conference when she was singled out in her red coat.

Even if someone doesn't remember an incident like that, because it was in a three-year-old's head, the brain remembers. It may remember in a confused way, but it can still influence behavior that seems very odd and anxiety-ridden to someone else. It is housed in the amygdala, a small but very powerful brain area especially attuned to remembering emotionally charged negative events in one's life. If you remember an event with vivid detail and know exactly where you were when it happened and how you felt, e.g., the assassination of John F. Kennedy, the Twin Towers, even memories from war that are considered now to be a part of post-traumatic stress disorder, your amygdala was definitely involved in processing and storing this memory.

Learning about this freed Jeanette from most of the behaviors that were a part of her life in the past. Even as an adult she would become a little wary when driving and saw a white cement truck.

That is gone now.

Instead, she will acknowledge by saying to herself, "Hi, cement truck—just go on your merry way."

One never knows the trauma another person has been exposed to unless they tell you.

First, You Must Conceive

Then You Must Believe

Then and Only Then, Can You Achieve

…Robbie

You don't "fall" in love
You build love.

CHAPTER ONE

The Beginning of Love — They Meet

JEANETTE HAD NO IDEA her life was about to change dramatically. Who in the world could have predicted this. No one in this earthly world for sure. She had decided she would give working with a strength coach a try in her quest to stay out of a wheelchair due to the disease she had. It certainly couldn't hurt, and even though she disliked gyms and felt a little self-conscious, she made the initial appointment with a trainer and headed over. She had never seen this *coach* before and had no idea what this experience would be like.

She walked in and asked the nearest person how to find him and was directed to his office near the back of the gym. He was immediately friendly with a great smile and welcoming handshake. They sat in his office initially as he explained what his training was all about and how he would proceed if she wanted to work with him. Around his office were several pictures testifying to his love of exercise science for many decades. There were also charts about nutrition, and Jeanette was delighted to see that he advocated what she had already been doing for several years. She began to relax and enjoyed how this knowledgeable man talked science, one of her greatest loves, and how his approach was different from others. He was obviously dedicated to his clients and took an individualized approach to helping each one. So much resonated with Jeanette that mirrored her own way of thinking and how she had been in her professional life.

Just like in her own practice, the first thing Robbie needed to do was assessment—to see exactly where she was in measurable terms so he could make a personalized plan based on her goals. It was mildly intimidating as he measured and recorded information, and then had her do some exercises to see her strength in various parts of her body. He recorded everything. She didn't know this, but he would later develop an entire plan for her based on what he found to build those areas of her body that would help her continue to walk and function as well as possible with the disease he already knew a lot about. This was a man dedicated to his profession.

When the initial assessment was completed and ready to be studied by Robbie, he said, "If you would like to work with me, there are two requirements. First, you must laugh at my jokes, and second, you must be my friend. You are not a client; you are a friend."

Robbie's Thinking

Gee, I like her. She is interesting and interested. Pretty too. She gets the science and embraces it. That is unusual and great. I think we are really going to work well together.

Jeanette's Thinking

That was actually fun. He is so kind and interesting. The way he does things, I really want to do the best I can. And so easy to talk with. I feel so comfortable with him. And he is my kind of good-looking. He sure looks a lot younger than he is. I like him.

Jeanette soon began to look forward to going to the gym. She especially enjoyed sitting on the bench doing some easy exercises while waiting for Robbie to finish with the client/friend before her. She enjoyed watching him, but most liked that he would usually come and sit beside her on the bench. Depending on both his and her mood, but mostly his, they would talk science, learn a little more about each other, discuss some important topic, and try to be funny. It was a delightful part of her day.

Robbie, at the time, was overworked. He had so many clients, and for a man that devoted himself to each and every one, his work in the gym was just a piece of the hours he put forth in designing each person's program, making charts to record everything—which he then used to continuously study and revise to ensure progress toward their mutual goals. Everyone was different and needed an individualized approach.

Jeanette would always get there early and sometimes would stay on to use the automated massage machine that she really enjoyed. She would often spend her free time watching how Robbie interacted with the other folks or even non-clients who would come up to him and ask a question after seeing what he did. The gym was a friendly place, and Robbie often introduced her to people or would talk about other clients and the problems they were having. He was intrigued that she was a neuropsychologist and found learning anything about the brain from her a joy. Jeanette would sprinkle in some information here and there, and he would seem to eat it up! She once talked about the amygdala and how it was activated especially for negative or emotionally traumatic experiences that a person could recall vividly and remember exactly where they were and how they felt when the event happened. Robbie was always intrigued with each new thing he learned. He began telling others about the amygdala and quizzing them so they would remember the name. Robbie made it into a game, and folks always ended up with a big smile when they could pronounce it.

Jeanette was learning a lot about Robbie just by watching him and interacting with him. His first rule was *Do No Harm* which was Jeanette's in her practice too. The most noticeable quality about Robbie at first was his kindness to everyone. Such a genuinely kind man. She saw this in everyday conversation and interaction with others in the gym but also recognized it as a natural component of his personality. He was not the *barking* kind of trainer at all, in fact, the exact opposite. He would use terms such as, "Do the impossible" to encourage one to put the most effort into something, he used positive reinforcement a lot and never made a client feel bad about anything.

Robbie would award *battlefield promotions* to mark substantial improvements and to lay the foundation for why a particular exercise would be amped up. There was a lot of positivity in his approach. For Robbie, it was important for each friend/client to know the *why* of each exercise he designed or invented for them. His knowledge of the human body was immense, and Jeanette and everyone else saw that when he started talking about the *why*, he could get very passionate about the topic. When he felt that way about something, Robbie could get rather talkative, sometimes not realizing that not all clients/friends were alike. Some embraced it, like Jeanette; others found it too much to concentrate on and just wanted to know the *how* of what to do.

After a month or two, Jeanette found herself thinking about Robbie quite a lot when she was not in the gym. She had no idea if he had any of the same feelings but did find him telling her things he had not likely shared with anyone else, especially when they were sitting on their *talking bench*. They got to know quite a bit about one another as their talks on the bench began to get longer and longer and more personal over time.

Why is it so easy to talk with him?

I really like her—she is a great person.

Gradually, they began to share some highly personal parts of their lives. This reflected the trust they both could see was getting strong. Trust is the absolute foundation for building love and caring for another person. Jeanette told him about the heartaches she had encountered in both of her marriages and on one occasion, told her good friend Robbie that she just didn't feel that she was *lovable*. He was so attentive, so caring toward her, and obviously affected by her revelation.

Robbie admitted to Jeanette that he often just didn't want to go home. Again, gradually, he told her that he hadn't had any intimate relationship with his wife for over twenty-two years and felt that she was constantly critical of him. He began to talk just a little about his own feelings, something he seemed especially wary of doing. However, because he felt so comfortable with Jeanette and trusted her, he began to do it. It was something Robbie had needed to learn to do. He had kept most of his true feelings behind a mask so he could hide them even from himself. Letting his true feelings out was a pivotal way for him to finally get to know himself and even like and then love himself.

And these two loved science. Jeanette loved the brain and how she had been able to help so many children and parents over the years. Many of their *talking bench* discussions centered on science and essential information. And talking science was fun. Pondering and solving problems or at least coming up with possible ideas to put into place was fun. Both Jeanette and Robbie loved talking together at a deep level. In the early phases it was more about ideas they mutually shared about life and what was important from a more scientific perspective. Jeanette just loved being around Robbie. Internally, she relished being perhaps thought of by him as being his *best friend* of his clients/friends. She felt the bond beginning to develop.

Robbie had his own thoughts. After Jeanette told him about the heartaches in her marriages, he had a thought that would repeat itself in his brain dozens of times.

How can these guys, her husbands, not see what I see? How is that possible?

On one specific occasion, she told him about the cruelty incident when the second husband left her crumpled on the driveway and told her to crawl into the house when she was ready. He became angry and told her he felt like socking him. It was the first time Jeanette had ever seen an angry look on his face. Most of the time when it was brought up in later great talks, he said he realized that would do no good—but there was already developing in him a need to protect her. Something he was willing to do.

There were some funny interactions too. On one occasion during a workout, Robbie was standing next to her by a workout machine and out of the blue, he said, "When I was much younger, I was a sex maniac."

Jeanette's reaction was instantaneous as she laughed aloud and said, "Well, tell me about it." Robbie was immediately embarrassed, but Jeanette was delighted. It would become a joke for all eternity. Robbie had no idea why he had said that. In fact, about two months later when she jokingly brought it up, he had no recollection that he had said it.

No way!

Then another rather unusual and potentially funny interaction occurred. Jeanette had a dream the night before and debated whether she should tell Robbie about it the next day at her session. She finally decided she should. As Robbie listened attentively, she told him, "Last night I had a dream—a very vivid dream, and you were in it."

Robbie looked at her inquisitively.

"We were in this place, and you were in this big glass case laying in front of me totally naked. You looked so glorious! I was trying to figure out how I could get into the glass case. There was only about a six-inch opening at the bottom, and I couldn't figure out a way to get in there."

The look on Robbie's face was a combination of shock, puzzlement, and a tad of happiness—all at the same time. Jeanette didn't know why she felt such a need to tell him about the dream other than she felt they were such good friends she should not keep it from him. Robbie then told a little joke and they moved on to the next exercise.

As she was leaving the gym, Robbie said, "No more naked dreams."

The interesting thing is about two months later when she brought up the *naked Robbie in the glass case* dream, he did not remember being told about the dream at all. At first Jeanette was rather disappointed, but then she became intrigued why Robbie didn't recall two very personal events—a little on the shocking side, as if they didn't happen.

Jeanette wondered if the first one, telling her that in his youth that he was a sex maniac, was an obscure way of flirting with her. She certainly felt that way at the time and was very careful in her response. However, it really made sense after years of their knowing one another when he surmised that at that time, before he really knew himself, that he tended to tamp down things he wasn't really comfortable with. He further thought that in situations where he didn't have control, he was uncomfortable. In such situations, he tended to avoid or not remember.

During the early days of Robbie and Jeanette, she found herself having a hard time dealing with the impending death of her aunt, who had been such a major part of her life. She loved her greatly, and she had taken the role of Jeanette's mother when she got her PhD and when her daughter died. She was so precious to her. Jeanette found herself telling the story to Robbie at the gym. As he always did, he listened so attentively and with such caring and concern. Robbie then did something no one had ever done before for Jeanette.

He said, "Let's pray for her…right now." He took her hand and walked her back to a corner of the gym that was more private. Robbie then said aloud the most beautiful, spontaneous prayer she had ever heard in her life while continuing to hold her hand. Something was changing in her relationship with Robbie. She could feel it, and Robbie could feel it too. Jeanette felt a depth of caring that she had never experienced before. A personal sharing as if Robbie was absorbing a part of her grief and making it his own. What an absolutely marvelous man.

CHAPTER TWO

First, You Must Conceive

ABOUT TEN MONTHS after starting to work with Robbie, at a talking bench time, he suggested to Jeanette that maybe it would be a good idea to do a class on the brain for his clients who were always commenting about memory issues. Jeanette thought it was a great idea but said she would only do it if it was totally free for the participants. Jeanette decided that the best way to do it was to have three sessions of about two to two and a half hours each, one week apart. That was necessary to put into place actual exercises participants could do to learn how to protect themselves as much as possible from memory issues. She also wanted it to be fun.

In Jeanette's mind it would be a way of bonding with Robbie as she planned to use him as a guinea pig and reference him repeatedly since everyone there knew him. In Robbie's mind, however, he wanted to learn—especially things he could apply practically for his friends/clients.

Jeanette had a lot of fun planning this seminar and how she would engage everyone and especially how she would involve Robbie in the proceedings. She wanted to maximize learning about the brain first, the *why* of the seminar, and then go into what would contribute to having a well-functioning brain whatever the person's age. Of course, she also wanted to discuss types of dementia and what happens to the brain since this was a mostly older group. More importantly, she wanted to teach what they could do to reduce the chances of having it. It was a lot to cover, and she wanted it to be interactive and interesting to all in attendance.

On the date of the first session, she began bringing in all of her materials and equipment and was surprised that Robbie wasn't right there to help her. It was awkward carrying all of the stuff, and the worst thing that could happen, happened. She fell.

A young man came right over to help her, not knowing what to do, and she simply said, "Get Robbie."

Within seconds, Robbie was there. He later told her that he was coming from his office, saw her fall, and literally ran to be with her. He also said that he recognized that he was beginning to have special feelings for her and the fall scared him a lot.

The class went great, and it was tremendous fun for Jeanette. A lot of her focus was on Robbie, and she would use his tendency to forget where he put his clipboard or his stopwatch or his glasses to illustrate certain principles. On both the first and second sessions, the class was given a homework assignment to develop a particular memory strategy using the tools they had been taught. Jeanette involved Robbie to quiz each of his friends/clients as they worked with him the upcoming week. They had advertised the seminar at the gym with a photo of Jeanette with the title, "Build the Brain," and of Robbie with the title, "Build the Body," calling themselves the Team.

For the last session, Jeanette had found a colorful picture of a brain and inserted all the things Robbie had to keep track of each day with the numerous friends/clients he had. It was also funny since the brain she had found almost completely spelled out his name within its confines. What are the chances of that? She explained to the class that those of us of a certain age have more in our brains than younger folks, and for someone like Robbie, with all he had to keep track of, it was like he had limited hard drive. Well, Robbie picked up on that right away and started to use the excuse of limited hard drive whenever he forgot something in the future. It was very cute.

Robbie and Jeanette started packing up everything to put back in her car. By this time, it was dark, and everyone else had left. After helping her, Robbie went to give her a slight hug.

Jeanette said, "I think I need a real hug."

Robbie looked into her eyes and, standing outside the car, quickly embraced her, and she hugged him tightly back and kissed him on his neck. This was a pivotal moment for both

Robbie and Jeanette. They would refer to it repeatedly in the coming years as they had the most extraordinary and deep talks anyone could ever imagine. First, you must conceive, then you must believe, then and only then can you achieve.

The weeks continued at the gym with each of them aware that there was a change in their relationship. Robbie commented what a great team they were. Jeanette was less vocal but inside was deeply aware of this man Robbie. Both had learned about the other through their conversations, their observations of their interactions with others, the way they interacted with each other, and learning how similar they were in so many ways. Jeanette saw Robbie as a good man, one who was kind, intelligent, funny, and wise but unhappy in many ways. He was carrying a burden that he was, at least in part, unaware of as he couldn't understand and sometimes acknowledge his own feelings. He had kept them hidden for so long behind his mask only gradually and carefully telling Jeanette—and no one else—what he was feeling. He really didn't know who he was.

Robbie saw Jeanette as a kind and giving person who had been hurt so much in her life by her marriage partners, coupled with the extraordinary grief she had suffered. He marveled that she could be as good a person as she was having gone through all of that. He loved how they could talk about things, be silly one instant and then have the deepest intellectual discussion the next. He was developing feelings for her that were totally new to him.

Some of the exercises he had designed for Jeanette required an elevated surface to do to avoid extra wear and tear. He decided that using the massage machine was an excellent place to do these. Jeanette loved going back to the room that was a little more private than the full gym. She felt closer to Robbie, although the door was always open. Robbie also found that he especially enjoyed his time with Jeanette there. He had to touch her just a little more intimately there. Robbie always asked permission to touch a person before doing so. Both could feel the electricity between them as they did these strenuous exercises.

Later they would tell each other what they were thinking and feeling while this was happening. Jeanette absolutely loved this time with Robbie. He was touching her legs constantly with her covered derriere on full view at the edge of the platform. Although the exercises were extremely intense, she couldn't help but focus on the feel of Robbie's touch. It was also more private and, therefore, more intimate. Robbie later admitted that he would sometimes become aroused as he was performing the exercise, saying to himself, "This is pleasant." Although he definitely kept this to himself at the time.

Robbie also invented an exercise especially to help her which he named the *Jeanette.* It involved using a large balloon ball with Jeanette moving slowly forward on it and then backward to increase the functioning of her knees. He would kneel in front of her, holding onto her sides so she wouldn't fall as she performed the rhythmic exercise. Although Robbie recognized that they had become very good friends, he was careful not to do or say anything in the public gym that would seem inappropriate. Clearly though his feelings about Jeanette were intensifying, and he was very aware of that. However, he wasn't prepared for what happened next.

Jeanette had been pondering her growing feelings for Robbie while at home. They were both in their seventies, and she wondered if this was just too old for love. But when she was with him, doing anything at all, she didn't feel old, she felt young. She was beginning to feel truly happy, something that had eluded her for decades. She knew the person she was. She had always been very empathetic, kind, and caring with an enormous amount of love to give. When it came to a relationship between a man and a woman, perhaps due to desire to rescue others and making the wrong choices, she had never felt real love. She had felt used and taken advantage of and even emotionally abused so she certainly didn't want to go there.

She had also suffered enormous grief. She knew that grief was really a reflection of the immense love she felt and had for those who had passed away, especially her daughter. The love between Jeanette and her daughter had been incredible and so very deep. She also felt that she had only survived by turning that love/grief into a positive by vowing to live the rest of her life like her daughter was already doing. She kept her alive with her every day, talked to her all the time, aloud, wore an angel pin every day she left the house, and took her daughter's stuffed dog, Patrick, with her on every trip she took, so her daughter could be with her too. Jeanette also had remarkable, no astounding, experiences of communication with her daughter that allowed her to *know* that her beloved child was alright. She also wrote articles, gave speeches, and even did a professional recording of songs she sang to honor her daughter. Like her son, her daughter remained an immensely important part of her everyday life.

With all of this to consider, Jeanette also didn't want to take the chance that she would be hurt again now that she was developing feelings for Robbie. She didn't think she could take it. Jeanette pondered and re-pondered, until finally she decided that she had to tell him. She just had to. Jeanette knew she would have to be vulnerable. This was something she had avoided for so long. She realized that she had built up some mighty strong armor around herself simply as a protection from this very thing.

So, for the next two sessions with Robbie, she tried to build herself up to take the plunge. Each time, she told herself, *Next time I will do it.*

The third day, she vowed to herself, *I will do it.*

After their session was completed, Jeanette watched as Robbie went back to his office. There was a bathroom just down from his office, and she went in there to give her some time to build up her courage. She then went outside and saw that there was a man in the office with him, so she turned around and went into the bathroom again. She waited about five minutes and talked herself into trying again.

She went into his office and stood in front of him. She was nervous and scared beyond measure.

She looked into his eyes. "I have something to tell you. I think I'm falling in love with you."

That was all she could manage to say. Robbie did not say anything. He looked at her intensely, never breaking eye contact. Later, Robbie told her that he heard a voice in his head, whether it was from his own thought or from another source that said, *'Do not look away'*—whatever happens, *'Do not look away.'*

And he didn't.

Jeanette had said it, and she felt she had to get out of there. She said goodbye and headed for the door.

Robbie sat there rather shocked and pondered what had just happened. He was so glad he had listened to the voice telling him not to look away. His first thought was of the courage Jeanette had to have to say that to him. He didn't think he would have that level of courage. As Jeanette pulled away in her car, she breathed a huge sigh of relief.

He did the perfect thing when I told him. He didn't say anything, didn't try to make a joke of it, didn't talk. He just looked at me intently with those beautiful, caring eyes and never looked away.

CHAPTER THREE

Disaster Strikes

ROBBIE AND JEANETTE began to share more and more with one another. Jeanette realized easily why she was feeling love for Robbie. She had been working with him for over a year, twice a week and had the opportunity to see him interact with many different people besides herself. The first thing she realized was that she totally trusted him. She knew that trust is the necessary foundation for true love. She also knew that he would never intentionally hurt her. As she watched Robbie and his interactions, she also saw that they shared the same values, not quite clones but very close. She also felt such respect for him and greatly admired the man he was. Jeanette didn't have to look far to see Robbie's kindness and true caring for others. He always put others above himself—but as he would say—he was still on the list.

Robbie knew how much pain and negativity Jeanette

had experienced in her life and marveled at the good person he believed she was. He also trusted her. Robbie had never opened up his own feelings to another person, male or female. It felt so good. He loved their conversations and the way he could communicate with her within the confines of the gym. He also had great respect for her; he couldn't believe all she had done for others in her life and her devotion to helping people in her work. He would tell her how much he admired her and began to use a word for her that she had very little contact with in the past—selfless.

Jeanette would be a little embarrassed when he said such things. She had always felt rather shy about taking compliments but had learned overtime to just say thank you.

Robbie had seen Jeanette's interaction with others in the Brain and Memory Class. He saw how kind she was to them, open in revealing things about herself that would make a point, and totally relaxed in a teaching role. Robbie knew he was essentially a teacher; and if you asked him, he would say that is what he enjoyed most. In her career, besides being a detective, much like Robbie, she researched, innovated, and developed techniques for helping students and taught teachers how to teach most effectively and taught parents as well. The fact that they were both essentially *teachers* really resonated with Robbie. He would often comment that nobody really *knew* him—who he really was. No one at home or in his family knew him—the man inside behind the mask. He so wanted to be known for the inside man, though he wasn't really sure who that inside man was. Robbie had been so self-critical that he really didn't understand himself.

When you look at the words *trust, respect, admiration, kindness, true caring*, they are the foundation for true love, and both saw the same in each other. Much more was to come, but not before an event that would totally change both Robbie and Jeanette and allow for deeper and deeper feelings and an awareness of the power of true, very deep love between two people.

On a mid-November day, Robbie found himself with a slew of clients/friends and also with a bad case of laryngitis. He was getting quite frustrated when working with the first of his clients because no one could hear him. Robbie decided to cancel all the rest of the appointments for the day and sent out texts to them. However, he didn't want to go home; he had told Jeanette already on several occasions that many times he just didn't want to go there. Robbie got in his car and started driving with no destination in mind. Along the way, he picked up some boxed wine to keep him company. He had gotten in the habit of doing this when under heavy stress.

Robbie just kept driving looking at the scenery and not paying much attention to where he was. He drove for hours, now in unfamiliar territory he had never driven before. Robbie wasn't speeding. He was below the speed limit, but it was getting dark, and he didn't know the roads he was driving on or even exactly where he was. Suddenly, out of the blue, he saw a stop sign appear, and he slammed on his brakes. This was a country road that ended on another crossroad. In seconds Robbie's car was airborne, going across the road, and headed for trees on the other side. Robbie had only seconds to brace himself with his arms straight locked onto the steering wheel. He saw the trees seemingly reaching out to him. Then he lost consciousness.

This was a lonely road with very little traffic, but someone saw his mangled car and called the state patrol. Robbie only remembered pieces of what happened when the police officer arrived. He needed to go to the hospital and remembered some questions asked, and he thought he was asked to walk a straight line. At the hospital, they saw extensive bruising on most of his body, but miraculously no broken bones. They apparently did some blood tests there. The depth of the pain Robbie was to feel hadn't started yet, perhaps because of the adrenaline he was producing.

The next stop was the jail of this small Georgia town. Robbie was charged with DUI and had to give them all his possessions: his wallet, his phone, anything in his pockets, even his watch. This was so humiliating for him. Nothing like this had ever happened to him before. His car was totaled. Robbie spent the night in jail, and it was a sobering experience. Although Robbie had been allowed to call home, his wife refused to come and get him. Finally, his adult stepdaughter came the next day and brought the bail money to allow him to go home.

Jeanette had been one of the appointments that was cancelled that Tuesday of the wreck. On Wednesday, she began to feel terrible pain throughout her body and had no clue what was causing it. She was also worried about Robbie; he had never cancelled an appointment before, and she hoped he was okay. She also had an appointment with him on Thursday and needed to find out if it was still on. With the pain she was feeling, Jeanette couldn't even walk. She stayed in a reclining chair for several days trying to deal with it. She called the gym; no one knew anything about Robbie except he wasn't there. She called some of the clients/friends she knew, and they also had heard nothing. Her anxiety level was increasing dramatically, keeping pace with the mysterious whole-body pain. Jeanette couldn't concentrate on anything else.

Finally, in desperation, she texted Robbie and asked him if he was alright and could he please text her back.

Jeanette is a very intuitive person who can sense discomfort and can sometimes feel the actual pain of others. She knew something was wrong. It took a while, but finally she received a short text from Robbie. He said he had been in an accident and was hurt badly and likely wouldn't be able to work for some time. Robbie was preparing an email to be sent to all his clients. So, Jeanette replied asking him to be sure she was on that email list so she would get it too. She did get that email with just basic information followed by a very long text to her alone explaining everything in detail— all that had happened to him. Robbie was in terrible pain throughout his body. He had massive bruising and injury all over his body from the neck down. Jeanette then understood why she had had similar pain all over her body.

He told her all about the police, the jail, the aimless wandering because he didn't want to go home, his wife refusing to come and get him, the fact that she had told him before that he was an alcoholic just like her first husband, and he had placated her by going to AA meetings for two years, although he never identified with the others. Robbie said he didn't think he was an alcoholic, but maybe he was fooling himself. Jeanette listened and then said something to Robbie that he would never forget. She told him that she had never seen any behavior with him that was suggestive that he was an alcoholic. Jeanette then explained that Robbie seemed to use wine as a way to "soothe himself" when under continuous stress. He needed soothing, and he didn't know how to be soothed other than drinking some wine. This memory and this word "soothe" Robbie would later identify as one of his most powerful memories in the story of Robbie and Jeanette. Jeanette also told him that she would have liked to be his "soother" in this situation and whenever he needed it in the future.

Jeanette was definitely seeing that Robbie didn't understand what a good man he was. He didn't understand his own feelings, tried to control them by not expressing them or not allowing himself to feel so he could cope. Outside of the gym, he was always questioning himself, contributing to his definite bent to be self-critical. He was particularly affected by being told repeatedly at home to *just get over it*, the lack of thanks or appreciation for all he did, and his perception that he was only there to make the money and do physical chores that needed to be done. It was rather a sad existence, in contrast to how he felt at work when he was helping others.

A little later Robbie told Jeanette that the date for his court appearance had been set for February in this town's courthouse halfway across the state. He told her that his wife refused to take him. Someone would have to take him because it was likely that he would lose his driver's license so couldn't drive himself. It took Jeanette less than five seconds to say, "I will take you and be there with you." She so wanted to do that for him.

At the advice of his brother, Robbie hired an attorney specializing in DUI cases. He vowed he would do whatever the attorney said to do to prepare for this court appearance. There were many courses with quizzes that he did online, many videos to watch, much information to learn, and requirements for people going through this. He wanted to do this immediately and have everything completed well before the court appearance.

He was also advised to get counseling which Jeanette supported. She called a professional friend and asked for a recommendation for a good therapist within the counseling center he founded. Arrangements were made, and Robbie began seeing him quickly. They worked very well together and continued for several months. His therapist also didn't think he was an alcoholic. From the day of the wreck, Robbie never touched alcohol again.

Robbie's pain was excruciating, and he could hardly move at all. Although he did not like to take any medications, Jeanette convinced him that this was an exception, and he needed to take some for the pain so he could move and think. It was quite a while before he could see any clients/friends even for a brief check-in. Just shortly after he began to do so on a very limited basis, he got the word of another significant event that would greatly affect the work he loved. The gym was closing. Robbie had worked at this gym for a long time, and the announcement of the closing hit all involved hard. He had to figure out how he was going to work and to find a gym where he could offer his services again while trying to recover from his injuries.

It was hard for Jeanette not to be able to see Robbie for such a long time. She missed him terribly, but they stayed in contact as much as possible. Robbie was having a hard time finding a gym that would work for him and his clients and frustration just added more stress. Both Jeanette and Robbie had talked about his insane schedule, and Robbie decided that he would never work with that many clients again. Jeanette suggested that he think about working as a concierge strength/rehabilitation trainer and perhaps go to people's homes to offer services. When he could later find a gym that met his needs, he could offer both.

As Robbie started to do this, he learned that many of them did not want him to go to their house because they felt they would have to clean it up before he came. He had never even considered this. Jeanette then told him that she had a big house with a gym area and some equipment downstairs, and she would welcome those people to use it. It was right next to her office, was clean and comfortable, and looked out over a lake. And the best thing was that it had a separate entrance, a bathroom, and was quite roomy. Robbie could not believe that she would offer her home to others for workouts despite any inconvenience it might cause. Jeanette, on the other hand, couldn't think of any reason not to. After all, the ones coming she considered her friends too. So, she gave Robbie a key, he worked out a schedule, and Jeanette and the others started seeing Robbie there. It worked perfectly. Robbie also saw other clients/friends at their homes and then found an excellent gym whose owner seemed to have the same philosophy as Robbie. Although he knew he could make much more money than the rent he charged trainers, he told Robbie that that wasn't his motivation—it was helping people.

Robbie suffered much guilt from the wreck he had had several months previously. Although he was the only one hurt, he kept imagining how he would have felt if someone else had been hurt or even killed. His self-critical tendency was still quite active, although, he had learned a little bit more about the good of himself through his interactions with Jeanette. He felt he had not honored God with his behavior, something he always devoted himself to doing. Robbie's belief in God and his personal connection were very important to him.

After the wreck, Robbie began reading numerous books—most of a religious orientation—to try to gain insight from them. Jeanette suggested that they read them together and talk about them. One night she was reading one that had been recommended to him and her reaction was simply one of horror. She couldn't believe what this book was saying and was deathly afraid of what it could do to Robbie if he accepted what it said. It was midnight, but she texted him anyway pleading with him not to take this book seriously and not to believe what it said. Jeanette was very spiritual and had been raised as a Methodist—the same as Robbie. However, her spirituality embraced many different concepts—but not these. She was truly scared for him.

They later met with all the books in his office at the gym—which had not closed yet. As they started talking about that book, Robbie explained what he thought it meant. They had found other books that seemed to resonate with both of them. But suddenly Jeanette had a thought.

What if I am not religious enough for Robbie?

It scared her so much, she began to cry uncontrollably. This wasn't like Jeanette at all. It was hard for her to try to tell Robbie what she was feeling. Robbie was kind and consoling, but she thought she should go home, telling him she didn't think this joint reading of books was working. Later that night, she handwrote a letter to Robbie explaining her feelings and offering to stop working with him if he felt uncomfortable with what she had told him previously—that she thought she was falling in love with him. The next day she took him the long letter, and after he read it, he said, "I don't want to lose you. No, I don't accept this offer."

The time was arriving for Robbie's court appearance in the small town he had ended up in after the wreck. Jeanette was so glad she would be with him. She knew how hard it was going to be for him. This would not be easy, especially since he had not even met his attorney and didn't know what he looked like, although they had talked on the phone. Jeanette met Robbie at the old gym and suggested that he drive her car to the town since they didn't know how much longer he could drive. They chatted as the friends they were on the way up, although Jeanette could tell he was nervous but tried to act relaxed and in control. Once in the area they had to concentrate on finding just the right building, and luckily, they found a very close parking space since Jeanette had a handicapped sticker.

They couldn't believe the number of people waiting to be admitted into the courthouse since they were early but made their way to the end of the line. They certainly stood out from everyone else there. Robbie was dressed in a suit and tie, and Jeanette was professionally dressed. As they got near the line, a gentleman, seeing Jeanette's cane, said, "Sir, you and your wife go ahead."

Jeanette had known she would be mistaken for his wife instead of a character witness who was also a psychologist if needed. Both later said they liked hearing that. The courtroom itself was old but quite roomy with the judge at the front with various legal officials strategically placed to take care of people paying fines or not requiring the judge's interaction. There were so many people packed into it, and Robbie and Jeanette took seats next to each other on the benches. It reminded Jeanette of the old *Matlock* TV show.

The only other people wearing suits were the attorneys clustered in the front next to the judge. Robbie and Jeanette tried to figure out which was his attorney, and they did choose the right one. It felt a little awkward for Jeanette; she wanted to hold his hand but didn't know if that would be appropriate. They first brought in prisoners direct from jail, and the judge heard their transgressions and made preliminary rulings. Then there were a ton of folks who had to line up after their names were called to go to one of the substations set up for fines to be paid for whatever they did wrong. This line would be endless as new groups were constantly called.

They had been there about an hour and a half when several names were called to go out in the hall and meet with their attorneys. This included Robbie, and Jeanette told him she would wait in the courtroom but to come and get her if she was needed. Jeanette watched people and began to think about Robbie and how he must be feeling, especially since the entire atmosphere was solemn and regimented. It was difficult sitting there alone and missing him being next to her. Time seemed to crawl, and she began to worry, probably irrationally, that he could have been taken to jail. She wanted to cry but instead maintained a put together appearance. She didn't know what the attorney would say to him. Jeanette wanted him to have it all over with today and not to have to face a trial or anything like that.

After about an hour, Robbie came to the door and motioned for her to come out in the hall. They found a bench and sat together as Robbie told her what had happened. His attorney wanted to take it to trial; he was sure he could make a good case against the police officer who had come to the scene and had made some mistakes. As Jeanette listened, her heart and her stomach began to ache. But then Robbie told her that he had told the attorney no. He would plead guilty. "I caused the wreck regardless of how much I drank. I will not go after a police officer that was just doing his job."

The relief Jeanette felt was palpable. This was the Robbie she knew—a very good man. She told him how she felt and introduced him to a new word to add to the many character qualities she had already shared with him. And that word was integrity.

He also explained that he would lose his regular driver's license for one year but would be issued a provisional license allowing him to drive for work and emergencies and be on probation. He had already taken all the classes and courses he would have been required to do and completed required community service as he waited for this court appearance. So, all that was left was going back in the courtroom and going before the judge.

As Jeanette watched Robbie walk to the front with his attorney joining him, she felt all his feelings. She knew she loved this man and felt his humiliation, remorse, sadness, and also determination. Jeanette wanted to hold him and comfort him, but he was not quite ready yet. Their love was on a path of growing, and he needed time to find himself, appreciate himself, unlock his own feelings, and see the good man he was. This became a mission for Jeanette, although she didn't tell Robbie this—yet. She was determined to help Robbie realize what a great man he was and to get rid of his self-criticism once and for all. Her heart was more full of love for this man then it had been the day before. Robbie later told her that this day was the exact day when their extraordinary journey to the love that was beyond all imaginings began.

CHAPTER FOUR

On the Road Toward Infinite Love

THERE WAS SO MUCH GOING ON in Robbie's life now. So much change. The gym finally closed for good after several *possibilities* that it would remain open. Robbie's initial inquiries into other gyms had not been fruitful as they did not fit either his clients/friends needs or his own needs. He decided to embrace Jeanette's suggestion of being a concierge trainer/rehabilitation specialist, accepted her offer of using her home gym as a place some of his clients could work out, and found a marvelous gym owner and facility for others to use who shared Robbie's philosophy of his major purpose in life of helping others, not for personal gain.

The use of Jeanette's home opened up more time for Robbie and Jeanette to get to know one another as well as friendships to deepen between Jeanette and the others who were coming to work out there. Robbie and Jeanette had never shown any physical affection to one another aside from her asking for a *real hug* after the conclusion of the Brain-Memory classes. However, both their friendship and beginning feelings of love really started to sprout when they had the opportunity to talk more and share things about each other. They were beginning to see how much they thought alike, how their values were essentially the same, the joy in conversing with one another, and myriad other details including what they would later describe as epiphanies. They realized this may have never occurred had specific events or circumstances not happened that allowed them to remove their masks and armor and to be able to talk so freely.

Jeanette never believed in coincidence. Her favorite quote is

Coincidence is God's Way of Staying Anonymous
— ALBERT EINSTEIN

The talks they had had previously at the gym, the growing admiration in actually seeing the good man Robbie was, and their true friendship were the major contributing factors to her declaring to him that she felt like she was falling in love with him. It is definitely not easy to let go of the protective measures we build in ourselves after being faced with adversity. However, both knew that love really couldn't grow as long as masks or armor were blocking feelings and truth.

In Robbie's case, he defined it as his *mask*. It was

complicated. You could call it a two-way mask. On the inside, looking out, Robbie's mom had graciously set the standards he wanted to meet by her own loving, caring actions. Robbie wanted to meet these standards, something a good man would do. He was constantly measuring his thoughts and actions against these internal standards, and when he felt he didn't meet them, he would become very self-critical. He would immediately berate himself, not seeing himself as being good, but bad and would dismiss all the good things he did every day, giving them much less weight than they deserved. He was living in two different worlds—the one at work where the real Robbie was there for all to see and the home Robbie, where there was a different man.

His mask was complicated further by his need to protect himself from behaving like his father did—it was the worst thing he could imagine in how one person could treat another. So, his mask also had to protect him from any feelings that would suggest anger, uncaring, doing any less than the very best he could, and expressions of unkindness. The worst thing Robbie could imagine would be to be compared to his father. He had received nothing good from his father—in any way—rather ridicule and disparagement. That is why verbal expressions such as, "You're just like your father," absolutely devastated Robbie. He didn't know whether to be angry, wanting to lash out but never doing, or ashamed. The one thing Robbie could later tell Jeanette with confidence was that it significantly affected his self-esteem.

Robbie's mask also protected him from the outside as he had to shield himself from his continuing feelings of disparagement or not being valued enough or appropriately, almost exclusively at home. To do this, he had to control all his emotions so that he could act in a way that would align with the personal standards he had embraced from his mother. By constantly controlling his emotions, he didn't allow himself to truly feel them. This included both negative emotions but also very positive emotions as well. Although Robbie was a very intelligent person, he had denied himself not only his own feelings and desires but the emotional growth he so wanted to have to be a happy and content person. Yes, Robbie's mask was extraordinarily complicated.

Jeanette had developed a mighty set of armor around herself. Its purpose was protection. She had been through so many decades of being taken advantage of, pretend love, nefarious motivations for marriage, lack of true caring, having to do everything herself, supporting others with no support of any kind given back to her, and emotional abuse. Her armor was thick, very strong and iron clad. She also was dealing with more grief than anyone could imagine. No wonder she needed such mighty armor.

That is why Robbie thought of her as one of the most courageous people he had ever met as he watched her leave his office and gym after she confessed to him that she thought she was falling in love with him. That was what he was thinking as she walked out the door. To take a chance at that after she had been through all she had with those two marriages.

Before his accident and before they had to leave the gym, in one of their conversations on their bench, Jeanette had told Robbie that she felt unlovable. Robbie later told her that that was the most ridiculous thing he had ever heard. He said to himself, *How could those two men not see what I see?*

He thought she was the most lovable woman imaginable. In those very long discussions, they would have later as their love grew and blossomed, Jeanette offered that the reason was both of those men were not Robbie. They didn't have the same motivations for love; they had pretend love in order to be rescued, to be taken care of, to be financially secure, to not have to work among others. They likely didn't know what real love was or felt like.

Robbie and Jeanette were about to embark on a new phase of their relationship. It would require an enormous infusion of personal self-knowledge for both, countless hours of self-examination and sharing of themselves, a study of love beyond anything they could imagine anyone else doing, and direct messages from God. It was as if their love went so beyond the feelings they had for one another but was also a research study and analysis to understand what true love really is, what is needed to have it, how these two people best express it, and how glorious true love really is. For people in their seventies, what a ride this was to be.

Although they didn't tell one another yet, they each had their specific goals for the other. Jeanette wanted Robbie to fully understand what a good man he is. She wanted him to better understand himself so he could not only embrace his goodness but truly know himself. Jeanette wanted him to understand his own feelings and to be able to express them without fear or judgment of any kind. She wanted him to be able to say, "I love Robbie" and mean every word.

Robbie wanted Jeanette to truly understand what a fantastic and good person she is, and that she would truly see just how lovable she is. He wanted her to be able to say it. He wanted her to *feel* cherished, protected, admired, desired, and valued for just who she is. He wanted them to become a team; he saw the potential of that during the Brain-Memory class and knew how glorious that would be. They both saw the potential for each of them, although they had never even kissed.

It was a little different coming to the new gym in Jeanette's home but quickly became a routine. The other friends/clients had their schedules, and Jeanette knew when to expect them but didn't want to interfere with their workouts. Jeanette and Robbie would do her workout, and Jeanette would often find herself in her business office while other workouts were going on. Often, if there was not anyone else scheduled, Robbie and Jeanette could sit on the couch and have discussions very much like the ones they had on their *talking bench* in the gym.

One day, while doing her actual workout, Jeanette decided to say something to Robbie she had never said before. As they were sitting on the floor, ready to do the next exercise, she said to him, "At some point I am going to need a kiss."

She was expecting him to contemplate this and sometime in the future—when he was ready, he would do it. She knew that Robbie had a lot going on in his mind, and it would take him a while to make his decision about where he wanted them to go.

To her great surprise, and to him as well, his response was instantaneous. He immediately held her and kissed her. Jeanette was rather shocked, she was just hoping for the future but absolutely delighted. Robbie told her he couldn't believe he did that—so fast. Jeanette explained to him that she didn't mean that very moment, but she sure loved how he kissed. Robbie, the analyst, tried to figure out why he had done that without even thinking about it first. Jeanette didn't care—she was quite happy. Afterward they sat on the couch, discussed it and other funny things, got silly, and kissed again.

As time progressed, they would do her workout, and he would save at least ten minutes at the end to *make out* on the floor as if they were teenagers. It was fun, loving, and delightful. Robbie would look for opportunity to stay longer if he could so they could talk, be together, flirt a little, and kiss. It meant the world to Jeanette. She had no love and affection or even touching for over twenty-five years. Robbie was not far behind. All of this time they were getting to know each other so much better—and as Robbie would say, "You know me better than any other person in this world."

Robbie was very good at it, although they both wondered how they would be if it went any further.

Meanwhile, both were being guided by their own missions for the other. Jeanette really wanted Robbie to understand what an absolutely good person he was. So, she wrote an essay entitled "What is a Good Man," printed it, and gave it to him. After he read it, she asked him to go back and read each point again. Then she asked him to tell her if he met the criteria. It was so eye-opening for Robbie. She could see that he was beginning—at least beginning—to see himself this way.

Jeanette asked him to take it home, put it in a safe place but readily available, and take it out whenever he needed reminding of what a good man he is. Robbie often needed time to read and re-read information so he could place it just right in his logical brain. Jeanette knew this and also knew that he would need much more to convince himself of the man he really was, but this was a good start.

WHAT IS A GOOD MAN?

A good man is first, someone that you can **trust**. He will have your best interests paramount in his mind, which will naturally include your safety, both physically and emotionally. You can trust that he will never intentionally hurt you, and if he has, mistakenly, he will own it and apologize, accepting responsibility for any misunderstanding. A good man never shies away from admitting a mistake.

A good man puts others before himself. He is driven by the desire to help others, to do something positive to improve their lives, to help them face challenges, and to bring a sense of peace to their lives. A good man shows and feels **empathy.** He can easily put himself in someone else's shoes. By doing this, he can naturally know how to interact with another person. His interactions are governed by **kindness. A good man** values **friendships,** simply for the sake of friendship and caring for one another.

A good man understands himself, engages in **self-reflection** to do this, and constantly is on a mission to improve himself. He has a deep set of **values and beliefs** and lives by the creed of **doing the right thing because it is the right thing to do.** This is what guides his life and interactions with others.

A good man is **passionate** about his work and devotes time and energy toward **learning** all he can to better his skills and knowledge. He recognizes that there is a greater purpose and mission to his life, embraces this concept wholeheartedly, and acts on this belief.

A good man accepts **responsibility** for taking care of and protecting those he loves. He wants and needs to provide for them and accepts this as a part of himself.

A good man, in love, will express his feelings **openly and honestly** and recognizes that love involves **both physical and emotional intimacy**, not putting one above the other. He enjoys sharing about himself and learning all that he can about the one he loves. He values and appreciates his capacity to love by bestowing upon his beloved everything he can do to cherish her. He realizes that love is an immense gift.

A good man has a **sense of humor** that he readily shares with others. He loves to laugh, loves to see others smile, and often keeps a smile on his face to bring delight to others.

A good man lives and breathes **integrity**. He doesn't make excuses and blame others but accepts responsibility when he has done something wrong. He embraces integrity as one of the most important values he commits himself to.

A good man takes care of his health and his physical self. He devotes time and energy to maintain himself so he can be there for others in the best possible way.

A good man is **fun** to be with and brings others **joy.**

CHAPTER FIVE

We Minister to One Another

ROBBIE HAD HIS OWN MISSION to help Jeanette. He wanted her to know how incredibly lovable she was and to fully appreciate the good person she is. They had talked so much about their own lives, hours and hours at a time, so they already knew each other quite well. They loved talking and sharing what made them the people they were. These talks were sprinkled with laughter, silliness, sweet gestures, and feedback from the other to offer fresh insights into so many happenings in their lives.

One of the things that Jeanette shared with Robbie was the death of her beloved daughter at age thirteen. Robbie cried unashamedly as he listened to her words. Robbie's ability to *feel* his own feelings was growing in remarkable ways. The part of his mask that protected him from denying his own feelings and therefore to begin to express them was going from plaster to tissue. You could see it happening. Jeanette told Robbie that she had planned on writing a book about the experience of losing her daughter but wanted to wait to write about the evolution over multiple decades. She had previously written articles that had been disseminated across the United States at earlier stages but thought that this would be something that she had never seen before in a book. The only problem was Jeanette was having difficulty starting to do this. She didn't know why. Robbie began to encourage her to write it, and when she asked Robbie to be one of the two *first* readers to give his opinion before publishing, she couldn't wait to write it. It was like a switch was turned on. She devoted herself to writing this book that would assist others, honor her daughter, and teach professionals how to really help.

It took her about five months to write the book and another three to four months to go through the editing, design of the book, creating the book cover, and the myriad other details that had to be addressed to get the book out there. It was a true learning experience for her. Occasionally, she would share something with Robbie that she had found that greatly affected her that she had forgotten about. Jeanette had kept almost everything over the years that had to do with her daughter—and she was so glad she did. For example, in one stack of things, she found a letter she had written to her daughter just days after she had died. As she read the letter, her heart both cried and sang, as tears poured down her face. She realized the immense love this mother and daughter shared, the beauty of how they interacted, the pureness of their love as well as the fun they had together. She also realized something very, very important. She *knew* her love for Robbie was as pure, deep, eternal, and beautiful as the love she felt for her daughter. Jeanette gave the letter to Robbie to read. You could see the emotion in his face as he read it, hear the sounds and sighs he made, and feel the love he felt for both Jeanette and her daughter. Robbie was learning so much about who Jeanette really is—and who he really is. Jeanette knew that this letter would have a pivotal place in the book—and it did.

When Jeanette finished the book and gave it to Robbie to read, she was nervous and hoped so much that he would like it. It was not in the form it would later be. Jeanette wanted this book to be aesthetically pleasing, with beautiful colors throughout, a remarkable cover, colorful photos, and quotations that were very meaningful and relevant to the story. These were just black and white words. She waited patiently for him to finish it, and when he did, he came to her and hugged her, then looked straight into her eyes and said one word, WOW!

That was Robbie—no better way to express his feelings.

Robbie would later tell her that reading this book was an incredible gateway to seeing and understanding the person that Jeanette was and is. Her daughter would have loved that. Actually, she is jumping up and down with delight. Jeanette's belief system has evolved through all the experiences she has had. It is profound, spiritually substantial, and embraces understandings and *knowings* that have come from her direct experiences and personal study. There may be others who don't believe in what she believes and has experienced, and that is alright. Everyone can have their own beliefs but should never, ever, deny someone else that same right.

Not long after her daughter died, Jeanette had a reading with one of the most famous mediums in the world. It was a totally life-changing experience. Certainly, one of the most profound spiritual experiences she ever had. She devoted an entire chapter to it and other spiritual experiences with her daughter in the book. As she was writing the book, she wanted to see how Robbie would react to it, especially as she remembered that one book she had read with him that so alarmed her. She had a typed transcript of the reading and asked Robbie to sit next to her so they could read it together and she could explain things as they went along. Jeanette still had some quiet concerns that Robbie may not think she was religious enough, although she was more spiritual than anyone else she knew.

As they went through the reading and Jeanette showed proof of nearly everything he said, sitting in the same room and in the same spot she had been during the reading, Robbie expressed amazement and certainly understood why Jeanette had felt this was such an important event in her life. She told Robbie that this medium had told others that this reading was the most powerful and extraordinary reading he had ever done. When they had finished, Robbie said that he saw nothing wrong with this reading at all. Especially at the very end, Jeanette *knew* that her daughter was there and actually playing with her dog. Imagine the feeling of that.

Robbie told her that there is a difference between *religion* and spirituality. He stated that religion was basically a set of rules to follow while spirituality embraces all forms of faith and belief and especially *knowing*. His own spirituality was growing with his relationship with Jeanette. He saw himself as spiritual and saw Jeanette as a spiritual being as well. As Robbie and Jeanette talked, they began wondering if their meeting and developing love was God-inspired. There would be a remarkable listing of *coincidences* if this was not so. They would learn more about that as their love began to grow voraciously.

One of the most gratifying activities Robbie and Jeanette did was to work together to solve problems and help people—they became a team. If a client/friend in an older generation had an issue that could involve the brain since Jeanette was a neuropsychologist, he would often ask her advice, and on several occasions, they worked together in seeing the client and figuring out the best course of training. Jeanette always loved research, and she would volunteer to study issues and learn as much as she could to inform others.

Both Robbie and Jeanette loved to learn; they were never satisfied until they fully understood what they were dealing with which could lead to innovative ways of assisting them.

One of the first was a man with difficulty walking, who mentioned that he thought he had had something like a stroke earlier but couldn't provide much other information. He was asked to try and get his records and any scans, but Jeanette just started listening to him describe his symptoms and where in his body he was having the most difficulty.

Jeanette then explained to Robbie the concept of neuroplasticity. She thought she knew where the stroke had occurred in his brain and why dedicated work to rebuild connections in his brain was a good course of action for him. Robbie was just fascinated and excited by neuroplasticity, and Jeanette knew a lot about it. Later, he would call it a *game changer* for him. Neuroplasticity has been know about for several decades, but surprisingly, many people who work in the rehabilitation field, like physical therapists, don't know about it.

The idea is to provide stimulation to an affected area in specific ways with the goal of building new neural pathways in the brain as specific movements or sensory information is transmitted to the brain. Once such new pathways are built, they can transmit back to the affected area, e.g., lower left leg, and improvement can occur in functionality. Not too long ago it was thought that if a specific brain area was destroyed—that was it—it could not get better nor could the affected area on the body. Neuroplasticity changed all that.

Two months later when this gentleman's records finally came in, the location of the damage was exactly where Jeanette had predicted it. After working with Robbie for a few more months, this gentlemen was able to again walk quite well.

There was a couple who became very dear to both Robbie and Jeanette. The husband had contacted Robbie to see if he could possibly help his wife. She had been in a nursing home for a year and a half, just lying in a bed unable to walk, very sluggish, and had difficulty talking or conversing in any way. It was obvious that this couple were so very much in love and had a remarkable relationship. In this case, Robbie and Jeanette were able to get records quickly and what they saw was quite alarming. First, she had been given a horrible diagnosis, a rare form of dementia, that causes death and likely led to her confinement in the nursing home. Second, she was on twenty-two different medications—many of which could interfere with each other and contribute to signs of dementia-like difficulty with the brain. Third, her blood tests had indicated Type 2 diabetes which had never been addressed for control through diet.

Jeanette researched the diagnosis and wondered if a specific defining test she had studied had been given to her to arrive at this decision. There was no indication that it had. Her husband had just made the decision to bring her home from the nursing home center; she had a hospital bed in their living room and a part-time nursing assistant. He also took her off all those medications. After she finished her research (Jeanette never charged for anything), Robbie asked her to come over to their home and tell them what she had discovered and her thoughts. After coming home there had been a great improvement in the wife once she was off all that medication. But spending that long just lying in a bed all day likely had caused muscular atrophy, and she needed lots of training. Jeanette asked her if she would mind doing that little test with her that was supposed to be the definitive test for that diagnosis she was given. This very sweet, joyful lady with sparkly eyes said, "Of course," and it was easy to do with her lying in bed. She passed it with flying colors.

Robbie began his work with her, and she was making great progress. What she really wanted was to be able to get to the bathroom by herself. That was the goal—at least to start. What Robbie commented on a lot to Jeanette was the love he saw between this husband and wife; they would banter silly things, he was so devoted to her, they were just plain cute. After months working with Robbie, she was almost there—it wouldn't be long. She would walk to the toilet. But then, she caught a cold, and it killed her. In order to take her home from the nursing home, her husband had been told that she needed to be classified as hospice. As such, professionals could give her nothing for her cold, and in her weakened state, it led to more serious problems. She was not showing any signs of dementia rather conversed easily and freely.

This just devastated Robbie. He had grown so close to her. And her husband was having so much trouble dealing with his grief. Jeanette helped him with this. All of this led to a shared interest Robbie and Jeanette were to have in the future—the problems with the healthcare system in this country, especially for geriatric patients. They would together study this and look at ways to educate people about so many older people who are dismissed or not cared for properly simply because they are old. This shouldn't happen, but they had both seen it many times. Both Robbie and Jeanette went to her funeral.

Working on difficult cases together was something both Robbie and Jeanette loved. It brought them even closer, and it was not unusual for them to have discussions about them for hours, coming up with new ideas and strategies. They felt that their brains were a lot alike—but there were differences. However, the differences complemented one another. Jeanette was a big picture person and very intuitive while Robbie was detail-oriented and needed to see and feel things before he would put the dots together. Putting those two brain/personality differences together was rather amazing to see.

Jeanette and Robbie also had a case they worked on together with a woman who over thirty years ago had been shot three times in the face by her then husband. This young woman spent seventeen months in the hospital, lost her vision in the eye where one shot entered her brain, and was paralyzed on one side. She was a beautiful, caring, and remarkable person whose mother accompanied her to her first session with Robbie. After she was released from the hospital, she received no other rehabilitation during those thirty years. Robbie had asked Jeanette to come to the first session with him since he was unsure whether he should take the case since he didn't know if he would be able to help her.

Jeanette asked a lot of questions to try to determine the pathways of the bullets as they entered her head. Both mom and daughter were such delightful people. Robbie already knew about neuroplasticity at this time, and they had talked about trying to ascertain if there was still connection between her leg and arm to the brain. So, Robbie started to do some manipulations, then got very excited and kind of yelled, "Jeanette, come here and feel this."

Jeanette hurried over, felt what he felt, and started jumping and yelling herself. "Yes, we can do this!" Both the mother and daughter then started yelling too. Hope filled the air in that house. So, another great client/friend. And she made tremendous progress while she worked with Robbie.

Yet another such case was a super guy in his eighties who came to meet Robbie at the gym. He walked in so stooped over that his head was looking down at the floor, he was bent over in a ninety-degree angle, using a cane to walk. It was quite a sight to see in this gym where a lot of folks were huffing and puffing lifting heavy weights. This was going to be some challenge for Robbie. But he loved challenges.

Of course, Robbie told Jeanette about him right away. They discussed the small steps it would take to get him to walk with a semblance to normalcy, and that it would take a long time. Robbie was so dedicated to him. He broke it down to the smallest steps of what needed to be done and got him strong. Robbie then focused a lot on getting him to stand up straight, without moving, and he got good at it as long as he didn't have to move.

People in the gym would talk to Robbie about all the progress they were seeing with this gentleman. Robbie would say to them, thank you but please say that to him, not me. One day, Robbie was in a quandary and was trying to figure out how to get Hal to stand up straight and actually take steps. He wanted to get him off the cane, if possible. Robbie and Jeanette brainstormed and talked and talked. Suddenly, Jeanette went into a weird looking trance-like state, which was really just her way of thinking and visualizing. She thought that the major problem was *anxiety*. Hal was so used to walking this way that it had become a habit. Whenever he took a step, he automatically reverted to the stooped over posture because the habit in the brain was a neural pathway in the brain that caused him to revert to it when he was anxious about moving. She told Robbie, "We have to build a new neural pathway to take the place of it."

Robbie was so excited! "Now we have to figure out how we are going to do that." Jeanette did her thinking trance again. "We have to take the cane out but without anxiety. I will come to the gym to help with this." They came up with using yellow ropes strung from two different machines at a beginning level of above his head that he would use to walk while holding onto them with both hands. Then they needed a word that Hal could use to cue himself to get in the standing straight up with good posture position. Jeanette explained to Hal that this needed to come from him, not somebody else, saying when she thought about it her first idea was marionette. She asked Robbie to hold him up straight by lifting up his arms while standing behind him. Then she said to Hal, "Now feel this feeling of stability with Robbie holding you up. What word comes to your mind?"

Hal thought for a few seconds and then said, "Puppet." So that became his cue word. It worked perfectly. Hal got better and better in walking the ropes in a puppet position back and forth and turning. Robbie would make gradual and small changes to make it harder but not to reduce his confidence. It was remarkable!

Hal even said, "I am more excited by this then anything I have ever done!"

The love between Robbie and Jeanette also included what they could do with their brains together, and the joy they both felt when they were able to create something that would really help others. They both knew their purpose in life and had been living it all through their individual lives. And they both had the same purpose—to help others. That is where their gratification came from.

CHAPTER SIX

Feelings as Words

ROBBIE AND JEANETTE were increasingly discovering that they really missed each other when they weren't together. Jeanette had made improvement in her sensitivity to not feeling abandoned or not cared for when her armor was coming down. At one time in the early days of using her home as the gym for her and others, Jeanette had been expecting Robbie to come back in and spend a few minutes with her after he walked another client/friend to her car. She sat on the couch waiting for him, and it was taking too long. She got up and looked out the window and his car was gone. She couldn't believe it! Almost immediately two things happened to her. First, she started crying and sobbing. And second, her armor started to rebuild itself.

She cried,

I can't be hurt again. No, I won't be hurt again.

Then she would have armor thoughts,

If he doesn't care about me, I am not going to care about him. I will just ignore him, so he knows what it feels like.

Jeanette hated these thoughts in herself. She could actually feel the armor beginning to surround her again. These were very familiar feelings to her, after all she had gone decades without love from a partner, feeling used and valued only for what she could do for them. Jeanette cried for two hours straight. She was exhausted, but her love for Robbie was too strong. She finally texted him and let him know what had happened to her, asking him why he had done that. The next day when he was there in person, he didn't want to do anything but talk to her.

The very first thing he did was take her hand, sit next to her, and apologize. Profusely. Although, he really hadn't done anything wrong. As Jeanette looked back on it, she realized that at the most it was a miscommunication. More likely, she had expected Robbie to read her mind. Here was a man that would immediately apologize for something, take the blame because he saw that it had hurt her. The last thing he wanted to do in this world was to hurt her. This was the antithesis of anything she ever had in her marriages. This was the beginning of Jeanette's realization that Robbie really loved her.

Jeanette then had an idea that would take their love to soaring heights, the deeper it became. She suggested to

Robbie that they start a book, kept in a certain place, and whenever they left each other, they would write little notes in it. Robbie loved the idea. The very first time they did this, the writings were short and limited. Jeanette had put a title on this first one, "What I love." Afterward, there was no need to put any title.

The first entry from the, **"What I love"** title was from Jeanette and said,

> The way you look so intensely in my eyes, with those Paul Newman blue eyes, with undivided attention, when we speak.

Robbie's entry after that said,

> I love your servant's heart, your willingness to go out of your way to bless others with the skills, abilities, and knowledge that God has blessed you with and totally unselfishly.

This book became extremely important to Robbie and Jeanette. And reading it was like watching true love blossom into magnificence. It was a visual representation, a timeline, of the growth of love that could actually be seen in each other's handwriting.

Another entry from Robbie:

> Thank you for all you have done for me. I am so grateful. You have given me much more ability

for me to understand me. It makes so much more sense. I have for years felt like a walking contradiction. Now I don't think that is true at all. I love you—and the person you are—not just to me, but for everyone God brings across your path.

Jeanette tended to be wordier than Robbie—most of the time:

You said something to me the other day that just cemented all the love I have for you. You said that our love and our relationship has given you joy. I had just written in my book that I feel joy again—something I never felt I would ever feel again. My joy is from you and our love. It is an immense gift. I love that you told me that. I am sorry I go through periods of needing reassurance from you. I have never loved like this in my life, and in my mind, I want everything. I crave it. It is hard. Yet one of the many things I admire about you is your integrity—your beliefs. So, I try hard to understand and support you. I also love how you tell me what you would really like to do! You are a contradiction in this way. And I love every crazy, wonderful aspect of you.

At times Robbie and Jeanette would express feelings that allowed the other to know each other even deeper than they already did. Sometimes, they would explain a misunderstanding or explain something in their personality that the other needed to know about.

Robbie wrote:

> *I so love our time spent together. It is a blessing every time. You are one of the most <u>selfless</u> people I have ever met. That serves as an advertisement for your heart. You are always looking to help others. I so admire that!*

Jeanette wrote:

> Love is so precious, so joyful, mesmerizing—and deep love is so elusive. I don't want my silliness (or yours) to get in the way. I'm sorry I sent that text. I should have just told you. Let's tell each other everything. I feel so grateful to have your love—to have you to love and give this boundless love to you.

Robbie wrote:

> *I feel us becoming closer and closer as we learn more about each other's character, personalities, behaviors, responses, etc. Every time I am privileged to be in your presence I am grateful and blessed. Thank you!!!*
>
> *Be careful on your way <u>to and from</u> the party. <u>You are irreplaceable.</u>*

As one advances in reading the book, it is like a window into the growth of love, in their ability to put their feelings and love into words.

Jeanette wanted to express her love and did it this way to Robbie:

> Sometimes it's difficult to describe what I love about you. It's such a big package. Let's see… I love your heart, your desire to help others, your unabashed willingness to give—not take and what I have discovered—an enormous capacity to love. I love your brain—the way you think, you listen, you take everything in and appreciate when something is important. I love your dedication to your work and how you can appreciate all the various aspects of the people you work with. Something I realize now is that I <u>need</u> you. For the very first time I actually need someone. I <u>need</u> your love, your protection, I need to be with you… to touch you… to kiss you, to feel our love—even though I'm not a needy person. It's a thirst for you and all you are.

There came a time when Jeanette went on vacation for a week, and Robbie got to feel what it was like to not have Jeanette in his life right there with him. And Jeanette got to feel the **missing** as well. They did text one another before going to bed, and that was helpful, especially for Jeanette. Robbie wrote in their book every time he was at Jeanette's house seeing clients or just staying longer to feel close to her.

Before she left, Jeanette wrote:

> You know I really believe there was divine intervention involved in bringing us together. And in "you" being the one to get me back on track to write my book. I just didn't know how deeply I would love you. And what this kind of true love really feels like. You are a huge part of my life now. I feel like I've known you forever, and I know you better than anyone in my life right now. I will miss you when I am on vacation, but I know I can look forward to your texts at night and what you thought of what you read that day. SIL

Robbie wrote in their book five times while Jeanette was gone:

> Jeanette, I am sitting at your desk as I am writing this. I am anxiously awaiting your return. I miss your face smiling and laughing. You are an emissary for _goodwill_. You always make me feel better. That is part of God's gifting. See you soon!

> Again, I am sitting at your desk, wearing YOUR glasses. I just finished reading everything, you have written in our book. I am humbled in response to your love! See you soon. Hope you have a wonderful

day. I am still in <u>hug deprivation</u>. I am looking at the couch we will be sitting together on soon. I need your touch! But be aware of the fact—I'm going to touch you back.

Robbie later told Jeanette that on one of those days he was sitting at her desk alone and writing in the book, he spent about an hour walking around the downstairs level and looked at every picture he could find. It was a way of being close but also a way to feel the person she was. He loved doing that.

Robbie's first entry after she had come home was:

Jeanette, it is wonderful having you back home. It was difficult to think of anything other than <u>your absence</u> for those nine days. I missed <u>you</u> way more than I anticipated. You seldom leave my thoughts at this point—and then it's not for long. I love you! Wow, I sure didn't see that coming, but I am very grateful that it did.

I <u>increasingly</u> love you as I learn more and more about you. I am so grateful for your impact on my life. I find myself <u>becoming</u> less habitually <u>stressed</u> and <u>self-critical</u>.

Thank you!

Jeanette wrote back:

> One of our songs on our playlist is "I want to know what love is — I want you to show me." I know now what this kind of love should be! Wow! This is so wonderful!

One night at midnight Jeanette went downstairs and wrote to Robbie because she was missing him so much. This was a long writing but part of it said:

> Our memories are so wonderful, and every time I am with you, whether we are just talking or doing something else, I feel so incredibly close to you! I know you so well. And I think you are amazing, and I am one lucky girl. There is a beautiful warmth to the love we share, so much trust and belief in one another. I know I can always depend on you. Like you said in a recent text, "you can get rid of the armor girl—I've got you." Those words meant so much to me. I love all of you—your heart, your caring, the way you think, the way you love, the way you feel, your quirky sense of humor. I LOVE ALL OF YOU FOREVER AND EVER!

Many times, Robbie and Jeanette would share in these writings how much their love had affected and changed them. Their relationship had grown and progressed from friendship first to a very deep love just by being with one another, talking and sharing everything without any fear or need for pretense, vowing to share everything with the other. They had become experts at communication and expression of feelings, although their physical contact was very limited and sweet.

Robbie wrote:

> *Here I am sitting at your desk again. Jeanette, I am so appreciative of your presence in my life. You very much make me feel loved and appreciated. Then those feelings turn around and cause me to love and appreciate <u>YOU</u>. The more I learn about you, the more I love you! I absolutely didn't see this coming, but I am thrilled it did. SIL!*

Jeanette wrote:

> I just love to laugh with you. It is so much FUN to be with you. And I love our science minds and how we can help other people. You are my rock, my protector, and I know you will always be there for me. That is so comforting and makes me braver. You have made me love and like myself better — that is a very big deal. I could never express the depth of my love for you. To try to express it would put limits on it — and there are none. It is beyond all imagination.

Robbie responded:

Jeanette, you articulate my feelings much better than I can. Your feelings for me are the same from me to you. I LOVE making you smile. I am grateful for your trust in me. I assure you that I will never take that for granted. Thank you, thank you for loving me!!! Every time I walk out this door, I begin to anxiously look forward to re-entering your WONDERFUL presence.

As their love deepened even more, Jeanette wrote to Robbie:

I feel like the real me — as complicated as I may be — just burst out of a cocoon and could FLY! We are so natural together. I may have a permanent smile on my face forever. I am so thankful, so grateful, totally amazed, and so deeply in love with wonderful you. And something very special happened at the end of our time together. It was the first time you ever used a term of endearment to me. You called me "BABY" without even thinking about it! I was kind of waiting for this and THERE IT WAS! I want to be your baby — even when I'm ninety-nine. Together, and in love, forever.

Clearly these two were so deeply in love, but they would be surprised and in awe as it continued to grow and grow—each day they loved one another more than they did the day before.

All of these feelings and insights were discussed by Jeanette and Robbie in hours of conversation—something they both loved and were growing quite skilled at.

Robbie let Jeanette know by writing:

> Jeanette, I miss you enormously when I am <u>NOT</u> with you. I am consequently very grateful when we ARE together. I LOVE YOU! There are a myriad of reasons why, but the bottom line is — I love you more than I thought I was capable of... for which I am happy, excited, grateful, and thankful. Thank you, thank you for loving me right back!
>
> I feel blessed by your presence in my life. I am in "WOW" mode as a result of your influence on me. I love you more than I can express! SIL!

A Little Note from Sages Ellie and Franklin

We have been watching these two for some time. Now, here they are in their seventies, and it is clear they both have learned what love is not and are well on their way to learning what true love really is and how it feels.

Both Robbie and Jeanette were realizing that their love was remarkable and more extraordinary than either one could have ever imagined. They both needed to make decisions. They both realized that their marriages were, in fact, quite similar in many ways. Each knew that they really didn't have love at all in their marriages, and in Jeanette's case, she knew that she had been taken advantage of due to her *rescuer* tendency and very strong sense of empathy. Once Robbie began to understand himself, allowed himself to feel and embrace his own emotions and learn what true love actually feels like, he realized that this true love was what he had wanted all of his life.

They both realized it was well past time to get divorces, and that neither wanted to live the rest of their lives simply enduring situations that were depriving them of any love, joy, and contentment. In both cases, there had been no intimacy for more than twenty-five years. Robbie had even lived in a separate bedroom for most of that time. Jeanette had not even had any intimacy such as holding hands or a touch on her arm for the majority of her marriage.

In Jeanette's case, she also had been subject to cruelty as stated and written by her attorney. Her divorce process took eighteen months. Her husband was motivated by trying to get as much of her well-earned assets as possible, as he had stated numerous times when divorce was discussed in the past,

"If you give me enough money, I'll be out of here."

That didn't happen for him. Despite the extremely stressful divorce process, the amount of work Jeanette had to do to protect herself, and the uncaring and cruel behavior of her spouse, Jeanette holds no ill feelings toward her ex-husband and wishes him well.

In Robbie's case, he came to understand that there was only wishful thinking love at the beginning and serious problems from the earliest time. Robbie really had no conception of what true love was at the time he married. He basically did what was expected. Robbie realized that their problem was they were absolutely not a good match; they had little in common, did not communicate well at all, thought very differently, and now that he had an awareness of how beautiful true love is, he knew there was never love. He had spent many years behind a mask, enduring his own feelings of being seen as only a provider whose job it was to make money, do chores, and to take on enormous responsibilities with little or no appreciation for all his efforts. Robbie did see positive qualities in his wife; she was a nurturing person to her grandchildren, but there was nothing between the two of them and hadn't been for most of the marriage. Robbie was determined to be kind, generous, and fair with the divorce, and he was. Since he had this objective, this divorce was much more amicable than Jeanette's was, handled with only one attorney for both.

Jeanette and Robbie also had numerous spiritual discussions about their beliefs and what God would want. They truly believed that God may have been behind this love they found and grew. They felt that God is Love and love is what God wants for all of us. God does not want people to live in misery, without love. When God provides true, deep love, it is a gift, a blessing.

CHAPTER SEVEN

I Know You Better Than Anyone Else on Earth

ONE OF THE MOST POWERFUL THINGS Jeanette decided to do in her mission for Robbie to really know himself and to get to know her was to introduce him to the Myers-Briggs Personality Test. Jeanette had already taken it and found it extremely helpful in understanding herself. Robbie knew nothing about it but was eager to take it and learn. As he was already learning about the *real Robbie,* he was even more intrigued to discover what he had not realized yet.

After Robbie completed the assessment, Jeanette scored it and introduced him to himself. It was such a revelation for him. It made so many pieces of the puzzle fit together for him. They spent many hours talking about it as well as Jeanette's personality assessment. Both wanted to learn as much as possible about each other.

Robbie's personality type was ISFJ which stands for Introverted, Sensory, Feeling, and Judgment. It is important to study it carefully to understand oneself and gain insight into past happenings and why we are the way we are. It is a tool and should be viewed that way. In Robbie's case, it was a game changer.

An ISFJ is usually known as a *protector* or *defender*. People with this personality type are noted to be unassuming, very hardworking, very sensitive and caring individuals who are capable and have a wealth of versatile gifts. They are gifted with excellent analytical skills and especially have a keen eye for details. They rarely seek recognition for all they do and often prefer not to be the center of attention.

The ISFJ personality, like Robbie, will drop everything to help others with a strong sense of loyalty and often have a mission in life to help others. Robbie had already shared with Jeanette that this was indeed his life's purpose. ISFJ's aren't settled with just doing enough; they strive to do the utmost they can, to be the absolute best they can. However, they are humble and tend to underplay their accomplishments. They often have a hard time accepting compliments, not knowing exactly how to do that. They don't work and dedicate themselves to others for recognition, rather simply to fulfill their purpose in life.

Even though they are introverts, they do have a deep social nature. It depends on the setting. Since they are so detail-oriented, they can remember details about others' lives and, therefore, can show up for others in their attempt to help them build stable and fulfilling lives. So, in certain settings they could appear to be extraverted while their true nature is introversion.

ISFJ's have many strengths. They truly find enjoyment in helping others and will use their knowledge and skills, incredible attentional skills and expertise to do just that. They are very observant individuals, a factor which can give them much insight into what others need and their emotions. These personalities have a need to get things finished and can be seen as meticulous and quite careful. They want things done to the highest standard; a factor they impose upon themselves.

ISFJ's, like Robbie, are enthusiastic, warm, and always ready to protect and defend the ones they love. They are viewed as practical but with a strong altruistic nature. They will do whatever is necessary by taking action to care for their loved ones.

The challenges with the ISFJ personality can involve being overly humble or too altruistic. They have a very generous nature so can be taken advantage of by others because of it. When someone else is not doing their share, they may have a hard time saying anything about it. They would just prefer to clean up someone else's mess than confront them.

Although they might try to come off as nonchalant, they are deeply sensitive to others' opinions of them. They have much difficulty dealing with personal criticism; they feel they are experiencing a personal attack.

A characteristic that particularly resonated with Robbie was this personality's penchant to repress their own feelings. This was a big one for Robbie, and Jeanette knew this. Especially when dealing with negative feelings, they tend to internalize their feelings (Robbie's mask). In certain relationships, these repressed feelings can lead to strong resentment leading to an outburst of frustration. Remember, Robbie's wreck when he just didn't want to go home after having to leave the gym since he had laryngitis.

Robbie's personality type tends to be quite reluctant to change. Breaking with tradition doesn't come easily for them. They may wait until a situation reaches a breaking point before altering course.

In romantic relationships, ISFJ's explode with passionate commitment to the one they love. They are intensely loyal, and the intensity of the feelings they have for the loved one really surprises them. Robbie stated and displayed this exact thing hundreds of times when interacting with Jeanette.

He would physically tense his muscles and say, "I just can't believe how much I love you! I have never felt anything like this before! I didn't even know I could feel this!"

The emotions of the ISFJ are deep, sometimes so deep it seems to overwhelm them. They often find it difficult to put into words—but they want to—to express how much their partner means to them. They show their affection in so many ways, every day, eager to make their loved one's day and life better. They have a fierce need to protect and care for their partner. Over their years of knowing one another, both Robbie and Jeanette really recognized this immediately, especially Robbie. They would struggle for just the right word to use and often laughed and would be silly about it. Both would generate special sayings, words or acronyms to put their love into words. Robbie *really* became good at it, which led Jeanette to often tell him, "You are so wise!"

Another interesting characteristic of ISFJ's in love, is that they struggle to take the initiative—at first. However, this can contribute to a feeling of being stuck—waiting for the other to take the first step. ISFJ's place tremendous value on deep, enduring relationships characterized by continuous connections and prefer long term commitment. When they have found that relationship, they are committed, a superb word to describe them. In a relationship when in love, they are exceptionally loving, giving, and supportive. They want to build and maintain a lasting bond with the one they cherish.

This personality type gives so much to their relationships that they can feel very deeply hurt when they do not feel they are reciprocally feeling enough love, respect, appreciation, and dedication in return. They may have difficulty breaking off from such a relationship due to misplaced loyalty, fear of change, or feeling that they have the responsibility to somehow figure out how to make it better.

The J in ISFJ, although it means judging, has nothing to do with what most people would assume by the word judging. It refers to the desire of this personality to be highly organized, to prefer planning and organizing tasks and information, and to live in an orderly environment. This would be in contrast to a more spontaneous way of living without care for such things. This wasn't an aha moment, but Robbie instantly realized why he had to clean up after everyone at home. The one thing an ISFJ can't stand is disorder and chaos.

This tool of using the Myers-Briggs absolutely helped Robbie immensely. All of it was important and enlightening. You could almost see the lightbulbs going off in his head as realizations came to him in their discussions and then understandings of Robbie and his life. The biggest, although there were so many, was Robbie's recognition that he was a *protector* and had been one all his life. He now understood why he had had so many fights in his youth as he was trying to *protect* other kids who were being bullied. It also helped him understand so many other actions—his need to protect and care for all his clients/friends and why his way of being a strength trainer/rehabilitation specialist was so unusual but fit exactly with his personality. He also recognized his taking on enormous responsibility at home with all the individuals living there that he automatically supported. And it even helped him understand his devotion and growing love for Jeanette and why she was so important to him.

And he recognized how he had repressed his emotions so he would not explode in anger at his home situation. This had caused him to forgo many positive emotions that he yearned for, was just beginning to understand, and wanted to feel.

Jeanette's personality type on the Myers-Briggs was INFJ. This stands for Introverted, Intuitive, Feeling, and Judging. The only difference between the two of them was Jeanette was highly intuitive while Robbie needed direct experience and observation in his environment in decision-making processes. This was also reflected in that Jeanette saw the big picture, while Robbie started with details and pieced them together—connecting the dots.

INFJ's like Jeanette are rare. They comprise only 1-2 percent of the general population. What sets them apart is the combination of intuition and insight. They see patterns and connections that others might miss. Frequently, they think about the future and are quite visionary. INFJ's have a deep sense of empathy, often feeling the emotions of others around them. They also tend to have strong personal values, to which they are very committed. Very frequently they seek to make the world better and are motivated by their own sense of purpose.

The inner lives of INFJ's are rich and filled with complex thoughts and feelings. At times this may make them difficult for others to understand. They also need time, as other introverts do, to recharge while alone. However, they want deep and meaningful connections with others. Like Robbie, judging characteristics mean that they prefer structure, organization, and planning as they live their lives as opposed to spontaneity.

INFJ's are referred to as Counselors, Advocates, and Mystics. They look for the deeper truth, beyond superficiality. At times, they appear to have an almost uncanny ability to understand people's true motivations, needs, and feelings. INFJ's are highly ethical with a strong sense of principles, beliefs, and values. Lying is considered by them to be morally wrong, and they will put forth much effort not to deceive other people. They are very unlikely to take advantage of others.

INFJ's like Jeanette are very passionate people. They seek a sense of purpose in life which Jeanette sometimes refers to as her mission in life. INFJ's will shoot for the stars and their own dreams. They are passionate about the beauty of their visions for the future. An INFJ rejects succeeding at another person's expense. Rather, they want to use their strengths and gifts for the greater good. INFJ's pay close attention to how their words as well as actions may affect other people. These are the ones that want to make the world a better place, and they will start with the people around them.

People with the INFJ personality type are creative and thoroughly enjoy the creative process. They will diligently look for ways to express themselves and think outside the box.

However, INFJ's are often quite adverse to criticism, especially if they feel that someone is challenging their core and most cherished beliefs or values. When this happens, they may become defensive, angry, or dismissive. They tend to be private but greatly value honesty and being authentic in interactions with others. They don't want to have to fake being someone that another expected—they want to be themselves. Although they are definitely idealistic, they may be prone to perfectionism.

INFJ's really want to do extraordinary things with their lives. However, they can burn out since they tend to be reserved and perfectionistic and can exhaust themselves unless they bring balance to their lives. They need to balance their desire to help others with good self-care and rest.

In romantic relationships, INFJ's look for depth and meaning; they deeply desire it. They have a vivid, vibrant imagination and can imagine the best, but they are also prone to unrealistic expectations. It may take them time to find a real partner—they want true love.

INFJ's as romantic partners are warm and caring, insightful, and value honesty. They will work in a very patient manner to find and understand their partners' often hidden desires and needs. It is essential for such partners to have shared values, authenticity, and care about integrity. Once they have found the right partner, they will not take it for granted but seek to grow their connection. Especially important for INFJ's are regular conversations that allow each other to see into each other's minds and expand their learning about each other. This can lead to a rather profound level of openness, without fear or the need to keep something from the other. Many people can only dream of this.

The depth of the relationship with an INFJ, when everything goes right, is very far from conventional. There is no fear of expressing love; INFJ's know that love is not a passive emotion but an opportunity to grow and learn, and they need a partner who shares this understanding. INFJ's are intensely passionate; they crave an emotional and even spiritual connection with their partner. Relationships with an INFJ are not for those who are shallow in nature or can't be committed. INFJ's love watching how a loving and meaningful relationship grows and evolves over time. They are fulfilled by seeing it expand and blossom.

As Robbie and Jeanette studied their personality types, discussing them frequently and in depth, they were amazed at how much they were alike. First, they had the same values—what they called being a part of the *good people club*. Both of them had the same mission in life or purpose in life—to help others. Both also derived their satisfaction in life out of doing that very thing—helping others.

Although both were introverts, they both had social awareness that allowed them to interact very effectively with others enjoying this interaction. Neither one of them liked meaningless social chatter and dealing with large groups of people. Both Robbie and Jeanette thoroughly enjoyed and wanted meaningful, deep discussions and could do them for hours. Both were highly interested in science and understanding why things happened, and both enjoyed research to continuously expand their knowledge. The two of them were lifelong learners and never satisfied with what they already knew.

Both Robbie and Jeanette were kind, empathetic people who would always strive to do the best they possibly could. They were also both very observant people with strong attentional skills who would carefully listen to every word the other said. It was important to both of them to get to know each other in such detail that they truly understood the other. Especially as Robbie evolved over time and embraced his own emotions and let go of his mask, both saw the incredible value of positive emotions to enrich their lives. And both tended to have difficulty accepting compliments, put other people before themselves, and maintained their high personal standards for quality in their work. Both Robbie and Jeanette are generous people who love being silly, making the other laugh, making even strangers smile, and bringing joy to each other. They both are givers, not takers.

These two both needed order and organization and found it difficult to live in situations without it. Jeanette was delighted that Robbie was a protector. Although she also had a strong need to protect certain individuals, being a protector was a fundamental part of Robbie's makeup. Jeanette had never had a man as a protector in her life.

Robbie and Jeanette were both highly empathetic people. They both saw that they were people who needed some alone time and re-charging as introverts. The connections they both wanted with themselves and with others were deep, meaningful, and honest. They both highly valued being free to tell each other anything without any pretense or concern about how the other would take things. They both knew that they fully trusted each other, respected each other, admired each other, and truly delighted being in the company of the other no matter what they were involved in. Neither one wanted to have any secrets from the other; they wanted to be fully known and loved for just who they are.

They learned that they were both very sensitive to criticism, especially from family members. For a long time, Robbie was self-critical—until he realized what a good man he is. Criticism from others hurt most if it challenged her core values and beliefs or who she really was, Jeanette, or indicated that family members didn't know him, appreciate him, realize his value and took him for granted, Robbie.

They both were very loving, passionate, authentic, warm, and wanting depth and meaning in their romantic relationships. They craved these things and recognized that they had never had them before. Both Robbie and Jeanette recognized the enormous value of their ability to have deep, very meaningful conversations that they never got tired of, even if lasting four hours at a time. They even desired and built together a spiritual relationship that was extremely powerful as they prayed together and built their personal relationship with God and received epiphanies and direct messages back.

They did have some differences, after all they were not clones. However, these differences were complementary to one another. While Jeanette was an intuitive person who saw the big picture easily, and Robbie was detail-oriented, carefully assessing them to connect the dots, they saw how putting these two thoughts patterns together would only enhance their ability to help others. They were going to the same place just starting from different directions. Robbie couldn't take any spicy foods, while Jeanette loved them. Robbie was a little obsessive about what he ate—nutritional and not for entertainment. Jeanette liked more variety and couldn't abide beans and some other vegetables. But they both valued nutrition and taking care of themselves.

If you asked Robbie what he most loved about his relationship with Jeanette, he would probably say, "I love loving her. I belong to her, and she belongs to me. I am ecstatic with our love. I love US—we are a team, we are merged, we are one. I would not change anything about her—not change any cell of her. She is my perfect match. We are love. She knows me better than any other person in the world. She is my WOW!"

If you asked Jeanette what she most loves about her relationship with Robbie, she would probably say, "I just love loving him. He is the most perfect man I could ever even imagine for me. Every second I am with him I feel joy. He is this great combination of masculinity, kindness, tenderness, passion, intelligence, romance, and depth of feelings. He knows me better than any other person in the world. He is my WOW!"

CHAPTER EIGHT

The Icing on the Cake — for Robbie

J EANETTE HAD ONE MORE THING to do in her quest to help Robbie see that he was a good man and how highly others thought of him. She decided to do a *roast* for Robbie at her house and invited current and former clients/friends of his to come and celebrate him. Although Robbie doesn't usually like parties at all, he agreed to come to this one since he knew everyone, and they were all his friends.

Although the invitation used the word *roast*, all the participants were filled in that this wasn't really a roast, but a celebration of Robbie and a thank you for all he has done for others. The party started out with an activity called, "What do you really know about Robbie?"

They were all asked if they thought Robbie was an extravert

or an introvert. The voting was overwhelmingly for extravert though a few brave souls thought he was an introvert. They were told that he is a *big-time* introvert, although he can look like an extravert in certain surroundings like the gym or in working with one person at a time.

All were then introduced to Robbie's Myers-Briggs classification as an ISFJ. They loved talking about what each of those letters meant and then guessing what each of those letters was Robbie. Everyone got J right, knowing how detail-oriented, planful, organized, and data-driven he is.

Then there were six different activities designed to elicit feelings or impressions they had of Robbie or required direct information about him. For example, there was one called "Ransom Notes" where pairs of participants had to use limited amounts of magnetic letter tiles to generate a sentence in a specific time.

One of the directives was, "Tell Robbie that you can't take any more talk about the scientific reason for doing an exercise." The responses were hilarious, and Robbie and Jeanette were designated to pick the best one as each team revealed their answers.

Robbie seemed just a little bit nervous at the beginning. Remember he thought this was a roast and was expecting to be raked over the coals. The next one, which was so much fun for everyone, was a version of "To Tell the Truth." There were three of his clients that were pretending to be him, introducing themselves by saying, "I am Robbie Walker."

Jeanette, as the emcee, then asked them specific questions, and each answered according to a script that had been prepared in advance for each one. The acting was superb. They had rehearsed their responses and mannerisms so it would be rather difficult to tell who was telling the truth. After the real, fake Robbie revealed herself at the end of the questions, everybody else wanted to know the answers they had really wondered about. They learned things like Robbie had been on CNN, and his least favorite substance in the world was *rayon* and why.

Another activity was called "Around the Room," which turned out to be an emotionally impactful exercise for Robbie. Each participant was handed a basket with cards in it and a writing utensil. They were told to say and write one word that is a good description of Robbie. Each person said aloud their word, and no one could use a word already said. Some of the words on the cards were:

Awesome

Caring

Passionate

Data

Inspiring

Enthusiastic

Selfless

Knows it all!!

You could see the emotional impact this had on Robbie. Then Robbie was put in the *hot seat* in front of everyone for an activity called, "Does Robbie Have Good Taste?"

Robbie is very particular about food and nutritional value. He was blindfolded and certain foods were put in his mouth, and he had to tell what nutrient it was and could say only three words. Robbie loves to talk about things he is passionate about, and this limitation was really hard for him. For example, he couldn't tell the difference between raw cheese and pasteurized cheese and needed lots of words to try to explain his answers, saying, "Well, neither one was spectacularly delicious."

Robbie was such a good sport! And when ice cream was put in his mouth, he erupted with a big smile. It was definitely hard for Robbie to be abbreviated. He kept saying "but, but, but" or "it depends," words that were not allowed.

The next exercise involved participants trying to give a good definition of Robbie's own vocabulary when training others, affectionately known as Robbieisms. They included, The Ask, Watch Your Breathing, Battlefield Promotion, Super Power, and Gluteus Maximus. Anyone who couldn't give a verbal description of what these meant was asked to act it out. It was hilarious and fun for all.

The last activity as everyone was seated around the room was for each person to share either a *funny incident* involving Robbie or something he had done for them that they most appreciated. This was extremely powerful for Robbie and very moving for everyone. Each shared how much they appreciated, respected, cared for, and admired the qualities exhibited by Robbie. There were a lot of tears and wet eyes, including Robbie's, but this was an absolutely beautiful, shared message of utter agreement that Robbie is a really good man. One of the most impactful messages was from a long-ago client who described Robbie as a totally selfless man. Robbie was so affected by this. Jeanette knew the effect this spontaneous statement would have on Robbie, and her heart was just filled with joy. He shed tears, but they were tears of joy.

With tons of food, cake, and other refreshments, everyone just enjoyed themselves and what this party had meant to Robbie. No one wanted to leave—they wanted this joyous celebration to continue. Jeanette was so happy. She had wanted Robbie to know how he was seen by others and how appreciated he was—and to *feel* it inside. She wanted to get rid of any self-criticism tendencies and for Robbie to truly say he was a good man and believe it. That had been her mission, and this was the icing on the cake.

Jeanette didn't tell Robbie until after the party that she had asked everyone to write a one-page letter to Robbie telling him about what he meant to them. She put all of these letters, descriptions, and photos from the party and what people had said there in a book for Robbie to keep forever. It meant the world to him.

Some small excerpts from these letters were:

"It goes without saying the times spent with the exercises, nutrition advice, godly advice, and many other topics have made us true friends.

"I love your passion for learning and teaching. You have helped me physically and mentally. I know you have given me more years to enjoy my life and my family.

"To say thank you really doesn't seem enough. You have been such an inspiration to so many people. You've helped them to realize they can get better and have a much better quality of life just by understanding how their body works and the things they can do to improve their body, mind, and spirit.

"It was also easy to see how others respected you and your gifts. The qualities that blew me away were your caring, empathetic nature, your knowledge and intellect, your constant desire to learn everything you could—not for yourself—but to be better able to help others. You are so passionate about your purpose. There is not an uncaring or arrogant bone, or muscle, in your body. I do believe you are selfless—a rarity that should be celebrated.

"But most impressive to me is the reason you keep doing what you do best—serving the body of Christ and your fellow human beings by being the best trainer and teacher you can be. Thanks for serving us in your unique way—so faithfully—for so many years.

"I'll remember you forever. We danced across the mirrored workout room, stood on one foot, and many other fun things. You made everything fun even though it was a good workout. As I watched you, you made all of your people feel special. I am so glad I happened to find and get hooked up with you for the time we had. And I so appreciate your care and good work. There should be more people like you. Age 93.

"You are so much more than a dear and cherished friend. You are a teacher, a listener, a cheerleader, a coach, and a healer. Because of you, at eighty-one I feel stronger and healthier as ever. I love you, Robbie, and I look forward to many more years of fun and friendship.

"Over the past ten years plus, you have become more than a trainer. You have become a good friend. When I fell and broke my kneecap, it was difficult to believe that the functionality of that leg would ever be the same. However, thanks to you, my knee is about 95 percent back to normal and still improving. I can't thank you enough for your expertise and never-ending enthusiasm.

"I am so grateful for all the help and training you have given me over the years at the gym. Your spirit has always energized me, not just at the gym, but in life. You are such an awesome trainer and friend!! God Bless You Always!"

CHAPTER NINE

True Love is Mind and Brain, Heart, Spiritual and Physical

ROBBIE AND JEANETTE were already very well-versed in their understanding that they thought very much alike. But it was more than that. Yes, they shared so many values, principles, their purposes in life, and analytical, scientifically oriented minds. They actually loved and had the deepest conversations anyone could ever imagine. They could easily go from discussing a neurological issue concerning a client to what romance really means, to Robbie's need to *see* the details and then connect the dots to Jeanette's intuition and ability to see patterns and know what needed to be done or what was true by imagining it. All of this could happen in one very long discussion. They seemed to be able to talk about anything with complete attention to one another matched by enthusiasm. Such discussions were fun! Not only that — they allowed them both to know each other so very well to the point of predicting what the other was thinking or simultaneously using the same words or phrase to express something. This happened so frequently that they just laughed rather than trying to keep count of the endless times this happened.

They also talked extensively about their own lives, the events that had taken place, the feelings they had had, the positive and negative emotions they had experienced, and easily put together what it had all meant and how it had impacted their lives. These were very deep discussions, often birthing *epiphanies* which both felt could have sometimes come from them but sometimes from thoughts put into their heads by God. It truly was remarkable. If someone had been taping these long discussions, it is likely that they would find them amazing. At least part of that depth came from their high levels of trust and the vow they made to each other to have no secrets, to tell each other everything without holding anything back. It was one of the first vows they made to one another and a very good one. Since the trust level between them was so high, they could easily do it. Neither one held anything back—it all came out. Doing this allowed both of them to understand not only each other but to better understand themselves. They cried together, they laughed together, they shared things unashamedly, they comforted each other. In one word it was *beautiful*.

But these two could also be very silly and embraced being that way. They had their secret sayings, acronyms they might use in writing or in texting that only they knew the meaning of. Each of these became a part of them and their love. Jeanette and Robbie loved giving names to things special to them, and it became a way of letting each other know how much they were loved. As Robbie began to understand the good man he really was and felt safe and *alive* by letting his positive emotions become such a part of him, he often found himself so excited to, for the first time in his life, be in love. He most truly loved Jeanette and *knew* that Jeanette loved him too. That is the most powerful feeling. Jeanette felt exactly the same. Here was this wonderful, good person who shared all her values, had high standards and principles, adored her and told her that hundreds of times, would often just lay next to her and stare at her, and constantly thanked her for loving him. Imagine what that does to her heart. Robbie realized that he had never really known what love is—he had only known pretend love. And this love just blew his mind. Jeanette realized the exact same thing; she had never known true love but had been the victim of her own rescue mentality and others who just wanted to use her for what they needed. But this love was real. It was the full deal. It was mutual, open, honest, so endearing, so affectionate, passionate, tender, gleeful, blissful, and using a word that they both used all the time—gave them both contentment.

Robbie and Jeanette would often re-live events in their love over and over again. They went a really long time before becoming physical. They had things they had to help each other with first. Robbie had to learn what a great man he really was and to embrace all his emotions once he knew himself. Jeanette had to learn that she was indeed *lovable,* and she had to learn that from Robbie. They reminisced over and over again about that time when Jeanette said, "At some time, I am going to need a kiss."

She thought that Robbie, in his way, would take some time to consider this, and sometime in the next weeks, he would do it. Instead, Robbie just reacted and in one second, literally, pulled her to him and kissed her. He couldn't believe he had done that—without thinking at all. He knew he wanted to; he later realized that this was telling him he really loved her. Just like teenagers they then found themselves making out after sessions. But they already knew each other very well and friends in love they became.

Then it took a while to *graduate* to making love. Jeanette was the first to say they were making love, not having sex. They have never had sex together; they have only made love. The first time was simply beautiful, no—exquisite. Which brings up a very important point. Both Jeanette and Robbie are in their seventies. Both had not had sexual relationships or much affection at all for about twenty-five plus years each. That's a total of fifty years. Can you imagine what that felt like? There are some poor souls who would say, "But they're old."

Both of them would laugh hysterically at that.

Robbie would say, "Age is just a number on a piece of paper."

Jeanette would say, "I have never felt so young in my life!"

When love is this deep, so real, so true, so passionate and two people are so deliriously happy, it is amazing what they are able to do. Jeanette would add, "Robbie would put to shame many men half his age."

Robbie would say, "Ditto!"

These *kids* really loved being tangled, skin to skin. As soon as they were together, each felt an overwhelming sense of contentment, accompanied by sighs and sweet noises, their *contentment* noises. Jeanette wrote a little poem to capture this beautiful part of their lives. Whenever together, they just had to caress and cherish each other with hands softly moving on each other's skin.

I love being tangled with you.

Legs and arms form an unending ribbon of love tying our souls and giving each of us peace and bliss.

I love that our minds are tangled like a mysterious web. So many connections, so many tangled together ways of thinking but just enough difference to bring illusion and the deep desire to understand one another.

We are tangled together in what is important to us—what we are here for. An intricate tapestry of colorful threads of natural kindness, caring, and giving with a sense of responsibility running boldly through the fabric.

Two tangled hearts. Each one nourished by the other. Hearts that are so happy to have found this love, this "knowing" that WE should be. Two hearts that feel so free to say, "I Love You" over and over as if we are pinching ourselves to remind us that this has really happened.

To be so tangled as to know each other better than anyone else in the world. To understand without having to say a word. To look in each other's eyes and see a depth of love never felt before. A depth of love never imagined until it was felt.

I love being tangled with you—forever.

On another Valentines Day, a remarkable event happened that both Jeanette and Robbie would *never* forget. Jeanette had found and ordered a sign about three feet by one foot that spelled out in beautiful script:

I Love Us

She wrapped it and gave it to Robbie, who immediately mounted it over their bed. He then gave her the Valentines card he had picked out for her. Robbie said that there were hundreds of cards, but he really wanted to find just the right one. He was pulled to one corner of the display and picked out the card there. The *very first* card he looked at. Once he saw it, he knew it was just the right one. On the front it said:

I LOVE US

Now what are the chances of that happening? It totally blew their minds. This was not a coincidence—neither one of them believed in coincidences. How did both of them give the other something that said, *I Love Us*. Remember, Jeanette's favorite saying is "Coincidence is God's way of staying anonymous." The printed saying in the card said:

> Love where we've been
> Love where we're going
> Love being anywhere,
> So long as I'm <u>with you</u>.

Robbie had handwritten in the following:

> *This says it all. We complete each other. I never want to NOT be with you. You bring "US" so much JOY! You make me so happy. You are the greatest blessing in my life! I ADORE YOU!*

Now this amazing coincidence would have been enough to mystify both Robbie and Jeanette until they saw the next thing that happened. They had increasingly developed their spiritual connections over time. Sometimes they prayed together, and Robbie often felt that God had brought people across his path so that he could help them. So, he was always on the lookout. They both had similar spiritual beliefs in the overall picture. Jeanette firmly believed that God is Love; that Love is all there is, and that love never dies. Robbie had a personal relationship with God and often called on him/her for guidance. Both of their spiritual beliefs were ingrained with a *knowing*.

The next day after Valentines, they saw a beam of light from sunlight coming in from a large window far away shine directly on the *I love Us* sign that Robbie had mounted over their bed. But it didn't just shine and light up the wall. It <u>completely and only</u> lit up the actual sign—the three feet by one foot dimensions of the sign—exactly. There was no reason something like that would happen. It was like God or a spiritual being was focusing on that sign and saying, I Love Us as well and validating their love. Both Robbie and Jeanette were in awe and shed a few tears. Every single day since then, they have looked to see if it ever happened again, and it never has. It was—and felt—purely miraculous.

Robbie and Jeanette were increasingly starting to feel that their meeting just the way they did was part of a plan that was orchestrated by God or a heavenly presence. There were so many coincidences that would have had to take place for any of this to happen. They began calling themselves *soulmates* because they felt just like that. They had dissected their lives, their beliefs, their similarities, all their emotions, everything about themselves to a degree that would be quite unusual in any other couple. Jeanette very firmly believed that every single thing that had happened to them in their lives, including all the negative events and grief that had to be suffered, had a purpose, a reason. She felt that those events had to happen so that she—and also Robbie—could learn from them in order to become the people they are. Jeanette believed now that we are all here to learn, to evolve our souls. She specifically *knew* that both Robbie and she were here in large part to learn what love is—and what it is not. When you know both, that gives one a much better perspective and understanding.

Jeanette also learned—and of course shared with Robbie— that you must always remember another person's experiences in their own lives and what that has done to their emotions to understand and forgive their behavior. We may be too quick to label a person as rude, uncaring, spiteful, vindictive, jealous, or any other negative connotation without fully understanding where they are coming from. A behavior of yours that would be seen by you as caring, loving, or helpful can be perceived by them as arrogant, dismissive, or unloving. It all depends on their own experiences in life and their emotional state. By taking the time to reframe another person's demeanor in light of their experiences and emotions, it becomes much easier to forgive them for a perceived transgression. That doesn't mean you should accept hurtful behavior from others, it simply is a means for better understanding that can affect your own emotional state. However, we can't control what and how others think and feel, and unless there is an opportunity to discuss and explore with them, we just need to let it go.

Robbie would always talk about it in terms of kicking negative emotions to the curb and altering your responses to reflect your own value system as your guide. He couldn't do this until he really understood who he was and acknowledged all his emotions. By doing this, he was able to embrace those positive emotions he knew little of until he opened up and realized that those feelings, like true love, were what he always wanted. He also realized that he deserved to have those feelings in his life as Jeanette did as well.

CHAPTER TEN

Coincidence is God's Way of Staying Anonymous

EPIPHANIES

ROBBIE AND JEANETTE would have their epiphanies as they had deep talks discussing topics ranging from their own histories and how events had impacted their lives, to the meaning of life itself. These thoughts and realizations dramatically influenced what they believed about themselves. Such ability to discuss literally anything deepened their love and their trust of one another to degrees likely quite rare. They began to understand why so many people are unhappy in their marriages and had missed the joy and contentment that can come from such deep love. There seem to be some absolute essentials for a good and strong partnership — for that is what marriage should be. They thought of marriage as a team, and in their case, they already were a team professionally and thought about ways they could spread the word about how fabulous true love is. Since they both have the same purpose in life, something they had recognized in each other very early on, they saw how they could put their complementary brains and personalities together to work with and talk to other people. What joy that could bring!

The first essential was *trust,* and both acknowledged that they had felt this with each other just weeks after they met. Without trust there really is not any hope for a good marriage. They also felt that *respect, openness, vulnerability, admiration, true affection, and honesty* were essential components of true love. They felt and showed this to each other every day through years of knowing each other. Openness and honesty go together. Both Robbie and Jeanette vowed to each other early on that they would not keep anything from the other—and they didn't. They also were extremely honest in expressing what they were feeling. If you can't be honest with the one you love, you will never have as deep a relationship as it is possible to have. To be honest, you also must show vulnerability—and that is sometimes very difficult especially for people who have lived decades with masks and armor to protect themselves.

Another essential component for an exceptional marriage, in their views, required shared values that were honored and displayed in everyday life. Robbie and Jeanette share the same values. When they talked about their histories from childhood to the present time, they became aware of how much they were alike and had displayed their honored values and standards from childhood to the present. When you talk aloud, especially when tangled, so many *epiphanies* occur that inform self and other of exactly who they are. Both Jeanette and Robbie realized that they both wanted to be *known* for who they really are. Robbie felt that until Jeanette, he had never been *known* by anyone else. The closest to Jeanette was his mom. Jeanette also realized that she had never been known either; there were friends or some family members that knew parts of her quite well, but no one truly knew her but Robbie. It is a wonderful feeling inside to be known and accepted for just who you are.

God and spirituality also played a pivotal role in the development of this extraordinary love. Robbie displayed interest in all the miraculous things that had happened to Jeanette in spiritual communication after the death of her daughter. He was truly amazed as he was acquainted with them and thankful that they had happened with her to build her beliefs. Jeanette strongly believes that God is Love and that Love is the most important emotion we should seek while we are here on Earth. She also believes that love is eternal and never dies. She has had personal experiences and her own truths to inform her. This leads to *knowing*. Robbie now also believes that *Coincidences are God's way of staying anonymous*. Since both Robbie and Jeanette are both attentive souls, with an openness to possibilities, they are very comfortable with this.

They have both received personal *messages* from God that their love is a very good and wonderful thing. They recognize after seeing all the *coincidences* that have allowed them to come together and experience such love that there may be a spiritual plan that brought them together, even at this older age. Both also see that all the things they experienced in their lives were absolutely necessary so that they could evolve into the people God meant them to be. It was necessary for them to truly understand love, to evolve through emotions that would be hard for anyone to take, to find the good in others and forgive, and to so deeply value the love they have been given as a gift. Every hardship, every loss, every event, and the associated feelings were necessary for them to learn and absolutely believe in the eternal power of love, and that true love should be viewed for what it really is—a blessing from God.

God is Love, and that entity truly wants love to be the most powerful feeling any being can have. He/she never wanted people *to endure* living their entire lives without love. God also wants people to appreciate love. What better way to do that than having them actually live through learning what love is not and then to be blessed with a gift of such immense depth and power.

Everything in their beautiful love story is either a blessing of coincidences and synchronicities or truly miraculous and guided by the ultimate knower of love. It is just too much to call all this a coincidence. Robbie and Jeanette have lived the coincidences, and they *know* Albert Einstein's quote is true. They have reviewed everything that has happened to them their entire lives and discussed all the meanings they have uncovered. It has been an immense process but an extremely valuable one.

Think of these two souls in the dimension of heaven who came to Earth to learn *what is real love and what it is not.* Think of all the so-called coincidences that occurred that finally allowed them to meet. Think of the similarities these two souls within the bodies of human beings share.

- Robbie came down to Jonesboro, Georgia, a place he knew nothing about, after almost being killed in the rayon plant, realizing he needed an education, and knowing he would have to pay for it himself.

- Jeanette lived in Jonesboro, Georgia, at the same time he came down from up north. They had even gone to the same dentist and likely passed each other on the road numerous times when they were much younger.

- Both were very independent and responsible from early ages. Robbie hitchhiked at age *seventeen* to Baltimore, Maryland, for a job to get away from his father. Jeanette started college at age *sixteen.* Both of them paid totally for their college educations themselves. By the way, Jeanette was born in Baltimore, Maryland.

- Robbie and Jeanette both set high standards for their work, stuck to their principles, and were willing to risk their jobs for what they believed in. They were not fearful of authority.

- Both were lifelong learners and researchers. They were never satisfied with what they already knew; they always wanted to learn more.

- Both Jeanette and Robbie had the same purpose in life and were both quite introspective about it. They both had the purpose of helping others.

- Robbie and Jeanette both received their *joy* from helping others. It was their work and positively impacting other people's lives that gave them gratification.

- Robbie and Jeanette both needed autonomy in order to do their best work.

- Both were mature at an early age and trusted themselves to set goals and plans to meet them. Both had strong persistence and dedication to their work.

- Both started out with a career in education and then in private practice. Both received the greatest joy in their professions by helping others. Robbie wanted to be a blessing to others as he helped them. Jeanette wanted to solve problems in order to help others. They were both very successful in doing what they loved.

- Throughout their lives, both Robbie and Jeanette were *teachers* of a type and always loved teaching others. No matter what their *title*, teaching was a core component of what they did.

- Both had childhood traumas that affected them throughout most of their lives.

➤ Even when very young, both Robbie and Jeanette trusted themselves to set goals and work toward meeting them. No one told them what to do—they just did it.

➤ Jeanette and Robbie were both leaders, and their leadership traits set examples that served as models for others. They both thought "out of the box" and brought that to their careers.

➤ Robbie and Jeanette shared the very same values and were known to others as very empathetic, kind, generous, and caring people.

➤ Both of them were scientists and loved analyzing situations, talking about them, making hypotheses, and in turn, helping others with their own problems.

➤ Robbie and Jeanette both enjoyed discussing their lives seeing through the rear-view mirror with insight and continue to love this to this day and probably eternally. They both displayed high capacity for introspection.

➤ Both were put in advanced classes in elementary school in their fifth-grade year. Although their brains and ways of thinking are very similar, there are differences that complement each other and bring much greater insight into situations.

➤ Both recognized the essential of allowing yourself to be vulnerable in order to deepen your love.

~ Both Robbie and Jeanette had experienced direct communication with God and those in heaven in their lives. Jeanette's were extraordinary and gave her a *knowing* that her daughter was alright and God was with her. Robbie encouraged her to write the book that detailed these experiences and so much more in order to help both professionals and the bereaved deal with loss.

~ When Jeanette told Robbie that she thought she was falling in love with him in the gym, he *heard* a thought that came into his head that said, "Don't look away—whatever happens, do not look away." He followed that directive, and Jeanette felt it was the exact perfect thing for him to do. He said nothing at the time but never lost eye contact.

~ Jeanette and Robbie would never have met except that she was told that he was very familiar with her particular and rare disease. Most physicians are not familiar with it nor are lay people. Robbie's former wife and several people in her family tree had the disease. This was an extraordinary *coincidence*.

~ Robbie had an epiphany that illustrated for him why he got into so many fights when he was a kid. He realized that every time there had been a fight, he only got involved because bullies were picking on other kids, and he went in to protect them. He also then understood why he felt such responsibility for others—clients/friends and family members once he understood his personality type—the Protector.

- Both Jeanette and Robbie, through their tangled discussions, learned the power of examining *motivation*. This is so much easier to do looking through the rearview mirror. Living lives without love allowed them to understand *huge* questions like why they both endured marriages without love for so long. The ability to understand why others married them and why they did so themselves, was so enlightening and fit exactly with their personalities and values. They then used this to see why in these former marriages, there was never a match and never a real love. Even with situations Jeanette endured of a very harmful nature, both were able to say they had no ill will toward their former partner and sincerely wished them well.

- On a Valentines Day, Jeanette had a wooden sign made for Robbie that said, "I love US" that Robbie hung over the bed, and Robbie had picked out a card for Jeanette that said the same exact thing. It was the first card he picked after being drawn somehow to where that card was located. The next day, sunlight coming from the adjacent room shone exclusively on the exact contour of that sign. It never happened again. Double *coincidences?* No way. Both of them felt awe and knew it was God expressing joy and love for them.

When Jeanette received the phone call that her son and daughter had been in an accident, she was working in therapy with a Delta Airlines pilot. She left immediately for the accident site. One year later, this pilot also lost his son, close to her daughter's age, in an accident. Jeanette went immediately to their house to be with them; she had also worked with his wife and son. She began her very serious work of helping the bereaved from then on.

Just shortly before she died, Jeanette's daughter won the role of a *spirit* in the play *The Secret Garden*. She was beautiful and angelic, dressed all in white in the play. Both Jeanette and her daughter relished the fun they had together, rehearsing songs while *lying* in bed, attending all the tryouts together, and seeing her daughter perform like the angel she was. The irony of her playing a spirit whose job it was to assist in the communication of the main young character, Mary—her daughter's name was Maria or Spanish for Mary—was so very apparent. In the play, Jeanette's daughter, as a spirit, assisted in the communication with the character Mary's beloved deceased mother. Jeanette's daughter was killed just three weeks later. Both her daughter and Jeanette had premonitions that something was going to happen. Even though age *thirteen*, her daughter asked Jeanette to sleep with her. Jeanette began to get messages from her daughter and from God, just months after the accident of a profound nature.

Not too long ago, while tangled and staring at and caressing one another's faces, Robbie gently and decisively said to Jeanette, "Will you marry me?"

Looking right into his eyes, she said "YES!"

Robbie simply erupted. Jeanette had never seen anyone more excited and, as he later called it, *explosive*. It was like fireworks of happiness were exploding inside him, and his body couldn't contain it all. This went on for a long time.

He kept repeating, "I asked you to marry me and you said yes!"

Jeanette had such a wave of love pour over her as she said, "*Yes!*" again and again.

You should know that Robbie and Jeanette changed the wording of the minister's oath from,

"Until death does us part" to

"Eternally"

But they kept—"You may now kiss the bride."

The End.

About the Author

DR. LYNDA (as she is known by most) lives in Fayetteville, Georgia, just outside of Atlanta. She is a neuropsychologist by profession and worked for over 40 years helping children and adolescents and their parents and teachers in her private practice and in school systems.

Neuropsychology is often embedded within her writings and continues to be a major focus in her life. Dr. Lynda is the author of two books, *Journey* and *The Story of US*, as well as many published articles. Although retired from private practice, she still consults on cases voluntarily that involve neurological issues coupled with mobility factors to help design strategies that will work, mainly for geriatric folks.

Dr. Lynda maintains two websites. Her author website is: drlyndaauthor.com and contains much information about her current two books, as well as some articles of interest and blogs. She invites readers of her books to correspond or leave reviews directly on this website. Dr. Lynda is also a noted speaker on many subjects including neuropsychology, grief, surviving incredible loss, spirituality and near-death experiences. A full listing is available on her author website.

She also maintains a professional website: drlynda.net which provides free information to educators and parents about numerous childhood issues.

Dr. Lynda enjoys being with her family, being a writer, photography, digital art, and most especially dogs, notably beagles and basset hounds. She knows her purpose in life is to help others and has devoted herself to fulfilling this purpose. She will always continue to do so.